Demonic Gospels

The Truth about the Gnostic Gospels

By Ken Johnson, Th.D.

Copyright 2013, by Ken Johnson, Th.D.

Demonic Gospels
by Ken Johnson, Th.D.

Printed in the United States of America

ISBN – 10: 149354778X
ISBN – 13: 978-1493547784

Unless otherwise indicated, Bible quotations are taken from the King James Version.

Contents

History of the Bible 5
Books of the Bible 10
Books of the Gnostics 21
Gnostic Belief 31
Truth vs. Demonic Doctrine 38
Gnostic Gospels 45
    Gospel of Barnabas 46
    Gospel of the Egyptians 48
    Gospel of Judas 51
    Gospel of Mary 53
    Gospel of Philip 55
    Gospel of Pseduo-Matthew 59
    Gospel of Thomas 60
    Gospel of Truth 63
    Infancy Gospels 65
    Protevangelium of James 67
    Other Gnostic Gospels 69
Gnostic Epistles 72
    Apocalypse of Peter 73
    Apocryphon of James 75
    Apocryphon of John 77
    Book of Thomas the Contender 78

Dialogue of the Savior	79
Epistle of the Apostles	81
Letter of Peter to Philip	83
Pistis Sophia	84
Ptolemy's Letter to Flora	85
Revelation of Paul	86
Sophia of Jesus Christ	88
Other Gnostic Epistles	89
Dead Sea Scrolls	99
Useful Extra-Biblical Books	102
Conclusion	105
Appendix A Modern Prophecy	106
Other Books by Ken Johnson, Th.D.	112
Bibliography	122
Index	123

History of the Bible

People often ask me, "Who chose which books to be included in the Bible? And why were some left out?" They have heard all sorts of things ranging from "King James added what he wanted to the Scriptures," to "Constantine took out some books of the Bible and changed others." They have heard of the gospels of Thomas, Judas, and Mary Magdalene, to name a few. Why weren't they included in the Canon? Did someone take them out or were they never meant to be included in the first place?

These are legitimate questions for anyone thinking of accepting Jesus Christ as their Savior and becoming a Christian. Let's start by looking at how we got the books we have now in the Bible, and go on from there.

How We Got the Books of the Bible

According to the Bible, God created Adam and Eve. They were perfect and sinless. Satan temped them to eat the fruit of the Tree of Knowledge from the midst of the Garden of Eden. When they ate the fruit, it changed them in some way so that they then had a sin nature. This condemned them to an eternity separated from God. God created a plan to save them and all their children, all of whom had inherited this sin nature, condemning them to hell as well. God's plan was to send Jesus Christ to earth to be born in a normal human form (albeit sinless) and to die on the cross in the place of sinful humans to pay the penalty for our sin. If we accept this, we become children of God and are given the gift of eternal life.

The Prophets
To implement this plan, God literally spoke to certain individuals. These people are called prophets. God spoke to Noah and warned him about the coming Flood and ordered him to build an ark. God spoke to a descendant of Noah's son, Shem, named Abraham. God told Abraham his descendants would be enslaved in a land not their own, but in exactly 430 years they would be freed and led to the Promised Land. God also told Abraham that eventually one of his descendants would be the redeemer of mankind.

God also spoke to Abraham's son Isaac and his grandson Jacob. Jacob's name was changed to Israel and his children became known as Israelites. The Israelites were indeed enslaved, but 430 years to the day after God made that promise to Abraham the Exodus occurred.[a] God continued to speak to prophets; and some of them wrote books. These books were put together in a collection called the Bible. Eventually the Messiah, Jesus Christ, came and fulfilled His mission to redeem mankind.

Modern Prophecy - Proof
A skeptic might say: "That's a wonderful story, but I was not there when Moses supposedly led the Israelites out of

---

[a] Exodus 12:41

Egypt. I didn't see any miracles or witness any prophecies fulfilled. How do I know all this is not just made up?"

Good question. Starting in the next chapter, we will see book by book how these were added to the Canon. Let's summarize it this way: these prophets did miracles and gave prophecies that all the people in their own time witnessed. They also made long-range prophecies about the distant future. These events and *all* their prophecies were written down for us. So far, since Israel became a nation again in AD 1948, we have witnessed the fulfillment of over fifty of these long-range prophecies. See Appendix A and *Ancient Prophecies Revealed*.

So, if the Bible has proven itself by giving us more than fifty very specific prophecies that we have witnessed in our lifetime that we can test by the history books, and tells us the only way of salvation God has ordained for us, the whole message of the Bible must be true. If the Gnostic gospels have no prophecy fulfilled during our lifetime and their story of salvation is *different* than that of the Bible, then we know that these Gnostic works are truly *demonic gospels!*

True prophets listed in the Bible:
Aaron (Exodus 7:1)
Abel (Luke 11:50-51)
Abraham (Genesis 20:7)
Agabus (Acts 21:10)
Agur (Proverbs 30:1)
Ahijah (1 Kings 11:29)

Demonic Gospels

Amos (Amos 7:15)
Anna (Luke 2:36)
Asaph (Matthew 13:35)
Azariah (2 Chronicles 15:1)
Barnabas (Acts 13:1)
Daniel (Daniel 2:19; 10:7)
David (Acts 2:29-30)
Deborah (Judges 4:4)
Eldad (Numbers 11:26)
Eliezer (2 Chronicles 20:37)
Elisabeth, mother of John the Baptist (Luke 1:41)
Elijah (1 Kings 18:22)
Elisha (1 Kings 19:16)
Enoch (Jude 14)
Ezekiel (Ezekiel 1:1-3)
Gad (2 Samuel 24:11)
Habakkuk (Habakkuk 1:1)
Haggai (Haggai 1:1)
Hosea (Hosea 1:1)
Huldah (2 Kings 22:14)
Iddo (2 Chronicles 9:29)
Isaiah (Isaiah 37:2)
Jacob (Genesis 49:1)
Jahaziel (2 Chronicles 20:14)
Jehu (1 Kings 16:7)
Jeremiah (2 Chronicles 36:12)
Jesus (Matthew 13:57)
Joel (Acts 2:16)
John the Baptist (Luke 7:28)
John of Patmos (Revelation 1:1)
Jonah (2 Kings 14:25)

Joseph (Genesis 37:5-11)
Joshua, son of Nun (Joshua 23:1, 3, 14, 15)
Judas (Acts 15:32)
Lucius of Cyrene (Acts 13:1)
Malachi (Malachi 1:1)
Manahen (Acts 13:1)
Mary, mother of Jesus (Luke 1:46-55)
Medad (Numbers 11:26)
Micah (Micah 1:1)
Micaiah (1 Kings 22:8)
Miriam (Exodus 15:20)
Moses (Deuteronomy 34:10)
Nahum (Nahum 1:1)
Nathan (2 Samuel 7:2)
Noah (Genesis 6:13)
Obadiah (Obadiah 1)
Oded (2 Chronicles 15:8)
Philip's four daughters (Acts 21:8, 9)
Paul the Apostle (Saul) (Acts 13:1-2)
Samuel (1 Samuel 3:20)
Saul, King of Israel (1 Samuel 10:10)
Shemaiah (1 Kings 12:22)
Silas (Acts 15:32)
Simeon Niger (Acts 13:1)
Simeon of Jerusalem (Luke 2:25-35)
The Two Witnesses of Revelation 11:3
Urijah (Jeremiah 26:20)
Zechariah, father of John the Baptist (Luke 1:67)
Zechariah, son of Berechiah (Zechariah 1:1)
Zechariah, son of Jehoiada (2 Chronicles 24:20)
Zephaniah (Zephaniah 1:1)

Books of the Bible

Genesis, Exodus, Leviticus, Numbers, and Deuteronomy
God performed miracles by the hand of Moses. God sent the ten plagues that devastated Egypt, drowned the Egyptian army in the Red Sea, and safely delivered the children of Israel to the border of the Promised Land. Numerous histories of the neighboring peoples record the manna from heaven, the destruction of Egypt, and the destruction of the nations between Egypt and Canaan. God wrote though Moses the five books that would become the beginning of our Bible: Genesis, Exodus, Leviticus, Numbers, and Deuteronomy.

Joshua
Joshua established the new nation of Israel in the land of Canaan. There are numerous miracles involving Joshua that occurred during this time, including the sun standing still until he defeated his enemies. Shortly before his death he made several prophecies. Once these were documented and proven to be one hundred percent true, the book of Joshua was added to the Canon by the judges.

Judges
Judges records the events from the time of Joshua's death up to the time of the prophet Samuel. During this time there were fifteen judges in Israel: Othniel, Ehud, Shamger, Deborah, Gideon, Abimelech, Tola, Jair, Jeptheth, Ibzan, Elon, Abdon, Samson, Eli the high Priest,

and Samuel the prophet. Each of these performed great miracles of faith. God instructed these men (and one women) and raised them up to lead the nation of Israel. They had supernatural strength, talked with angels, had dreams and visions, and overcame seemingly insurmountable obstacles.

Ruth
Since the book of Ruth illustrates the purpose of the "kinsman redeemer," which explains how the Messiah would bring salvation, it was placed in the Canon by the prophets.

First and Second Samuel
These two books were primarily written by the Holy Spirit though the hand of the prophet Samuel and were completed by other prophets. They record the miraculous events that brought Samuel into power. One of the Prophet Samuel's prophecies was that the throne of David would be established forever (through the Messiah, 2 Samuel 7:12-16). In these two books we also see the prophets Gad and Nathan.

First and Second Kings
In these historical records of the kings of the nations of Israel and Judah, we see Elijah the prophet arise. Elijah formed the first "school of the prophets" to record and teach prophecy to everyone who wished to know God. He performed many miracles and gave prophecies including the exact day he would be taken to heaven. On the day of his catching away, his disciple Elisha asked and received

Demonic Gospels

a double portion of Elijah's anointing. Second Kings records that Elisha did twice as many miracles as Elijah did. We also see the prophet Iddo and others in these books.

First and Second Chronicles
In these historical records we see prophets like Micaiah who warned King Ahab of defeat.

Ezra and Nehemiah
Both Ezra and Nehemiah saw the fulfillment of the prophecies that Israel would return to her land. They recorded those events and added the wisdom books of Job, Psalms, Proverbs, Ecclesiastes, and the Song of Solomon to the Canon. They also added the major and minor prophets to the Canon.

Psalms
The Psalms contain many embedded prophecies about the Messiah: He would be the only begotten Son of God (2); His incarnation (8); His resurrection (16, 40); His future coronation (21); His crucifixion (22); not one of His bones would be broken (34); He would be falsely accused (35); He would be betrayed by a friend (41); He would be God incarnate (45); He would ascend (68); and He would be a Melchizedekian priest (110). There are also other prophecies: another would take the place of Judas (109); our eternal life and the Rapture (61); a future Israeli war (83); and the future return of the Spanish Jews to colonize the Negev (126).

Isaiah

Isaiah is the first major prophet. He records numerous prophecies about the first and second comings of the Messiah. He records the fact that the Messiah would be born of a virgin and be God incarnate (7-8), be preceded by John the Baptist (40), would be visited by the Magi and shepherds (60), suffer and die on the cross (53), and numerous other events in the life of Jesus Christ. Isaiah predicted the Medes and Persians would take Babylon (21), he predicted Cyrus by name and details of how he would take the city (45). He did all of this hundreds of years before Cyrus was born! He prophesied the destruction of Tyre in great detail (23), that Israel would be exiled twice (28), the Messiah would resurrect and the temple would be destroyed (28), that Israel would be brought back into their land by the British (60), the outcome of the 1967 war (19), and the yet future destruction of Damascus (17). Isaiah prophesied about the Tribulation period (24, 33), the Millennium (25, 32), and much more.

Jeremiah and Lamentations

Jeremiah predicted many local prophecies for the people of Judah at that time. He predicted the seventy-year captivity of the Jews in Babylon (25) and the new covenant that the Messiah would bring (31). The book of Lamentations shows that the prophecies of the destruction of Solomon's temple actually took place.

Demonic Gospels

Ezekiel

The prophet Ezekiel predicted the return of Israel in 1948 (37) and the future invasion of armies from the North (Russia) and the army's destruction (38-39). He describes the Millennial temple in great detail (40-48). He gives the most amazing prophecy of Tyre's destruction by Nebuchadnezzar and Alexander the Great (26). He records Satan's fall and the fall of the Antichrist (28). Ezekiel predicts Egypt becoming desolate for forty years (29). He predicted the destruction of Petra which occurred in AD 622 (35).

Daniel

The prophet Daniel accurately predicted the fall of the Babylonian kingdom, the rise of the Persian, Greek, and the Roman Empires, and the split of the Greek kingdom into four smaller kingdoms (2). He predicted the exact date of the Messiah's first coming, the destruction of the temple, and the dispersion of Israel (9). Daniel then predicted the various wars in startling detail which led up to the Roman conquest of Israel and the eventual destruction of the temple. He predicted the time of Israel's return, the rebuilding of the temple, and the coming of the Antichrist (11). He also details the Rapture and the Tribulation period and the number of days from one event to another (12)

The twelve minor prophets

Hosea

This prophet predicted the time of the Gentiles becoming the "sons of God" which was the day of Pentecost, after which, Israel would wander among the nations until the time of her return, approximately two days (or two thousand years) later. They would rebuild their nation and eventually have teraphim, or idols, again in their land.

Joel

The prophet Joel predicted the outpouring of the Holy Spirit on the Day of Pentecost. He also predicted events that will happen in the tribulation period, the intense destruction of the locusts, the attack of the northern army, and the fire judgments. He even gives veiled references to the Rapture and tells of a future time when Egypt will lie desolate for forty years.

Amos

Amos prophesied the destruction of several nations. These were fulfilled a few hundred years later by Nebuchadnezzar and Alexander the Great. He predicted the darkness at noon which would foreshadow the crucifixion of Jesus Christ, the church restoring the tabernacle of David, and the scattering of Israel among the nations. He taught that there would be only be two returns to the land by Israel and how to correctly understand the Biblical prophecies. He also predicted that in the last days there would be constant planting and

Demonic Gospels

reaping in the land of Israel and that the ruins in Israel would be rebuilt.

Obadiah

This prophet predicted the fall of Edom, which occurred in AD 625. He predicted that before the Day of the Lord occurs the Israelites will possess all of the coast of Israel from the Gaza strip to Sarafand, Lebanon. He also predicted that the tribe of Benjamin will return and Jews will colonize the Negev desert.

Micah

Micah predicted the Messiah would be born in the town of Bethlehem, and that Israel would be forsaken and laid waste because it rejected the Messiah. He also predicted that Jerusalem would be plowed under. This was fulfilled in AD 71. He also recorded that Israel would be restored, which took place in AD 1948. He predicted eight wars between Israel and Syria in between the time of their rebirth in 1948 and the time the Messiah returns to establish His kingdom on earth.

Nahum

Nahum predicted the fall of Nineveh and the entire Assyrian empire. This took place in 612 BC.

Habakkuk

Habakkuk prophesied the destruction of Judah by the Babylonians and Judah's captivity. He also recorded what is known as a musical prophecy, in the third chapter which also contains three riddles.

Zephaniah

This prophet predicted Israel's current land borders and the Gaza situation of modern Israel. He predicted the coming destruction of the nation of Jordan, the Rapture, Hebrew being the one world language after the return of Jesus Christ to earth, and he predicted a very special gift Ethiopia will give to Jerusalem when the Messiah begins His reign.

Haggai

Haggai gave predictions for his time, but also predicted the laying of the foundation stone of the next Temple to be on the eve of Hanukah, and the Second Coming of our Lord to establish His kingdom.

Zechariah

The prophet Zechariah had eight visions in one night. They included prophecies for his time and ones that have recently occurred, like Jerusalem growing beyond its old city walls, and the coming of an age of grace. He predicted the Messiah would come to Jerusalem riding on a donkey, and His being betrayed for thirty pieces of silver. He also prophesied about the Antichrist and the Tribulation.

Malachi

Malachi predicted John the Baptist would be the forerunner of the Messiah, the coming of Elijah the prophet, the Tribulation period, and that Jesus would heal many using the tassels of His prayer shawl.

Demonic Gospels

Matthew, Mark, and Luke
These three gospels tell the story of how Jesus, the Christ, came and fulfilled over one hundred prophecies in the thirty-three-and-a-half years He was on earth. They also record His predictions about the end times in Matthew 24, Luke 21, and Mark 13.

John
The gospel of John goes to great lengths teaching Jesus' divinity, His ministry while He was here on earth, and the only way of Salvation.

Acts
The book of Acts gives a detailed record of what God did through the hands of the apostles. It starts with the ascension of Christ and the day of Pentecost and goes though the ministry of Peter and Paul. It records their miracles and teaches us how to understand the Old Testament prophecies.

Romans through Hebrews
The New Testament epistles of Romans, First and Second Corinthians, Galatians, Ephesians, Philippians, Colossians, First and Second Timothy, Titus, First and Second Thessalonians, Philemon, and Hebrews were written by the apostle Paul. Paul wrote these thirteen books to teach us about God and how He wants us to live, along with the purpose of the church. In the books of First and Second Thessalonians, Paul teaches about the events leading up to the Rapture of the church and the Great Tribulation. Between Daniel and Paul there are over

eighty prophecies about the Tribulation and the Antichrist.

James
James is a book about wisdom much like the Old Testament wisdom books of Psalms, Proverbs, Ecclesiastes, and the Song of Solomon. Some of these books contain veiled prophecies that the most skilled reader will have trouble deciphering.

First and Second Peter
The apostle Peter wrote these two epistles. They teach about the apostasy that will form in the last days and the destruction and re-creation of the earth. They predict the church abandoning the clear teaching of creationism for evolution.

First, Second, and Third John
In these three epistles the apostle John teaches exactly who Jesus was, what He did, and the prophecies He fulfilled. John was an eyewitness of these events. Second John even tells of Jesus's physical return to earth.

Jude
Jude reminds us of how the angels and pre-flood world sinned. The Gnostic cults of his day were leading people astray. He describes how we can tell the difference between true men of God and liars.

Demonic Gospels

Revelation

The first three chapters contain the introduction to the book and prophecies dealing with seven churches. When the prediction about these seven churches proved to be one hundred percent correct, the disciples of the apostles knew this book was to be added to the canon of Scripture to complete it. The remaining predictions are veiled prophecies about the Great Tribulation and the Millennial reign of Jesus Christ.

Conclusion

It should be obvious to all that these books prove themselves inspired by God because of the accuracy of the predictions made thousands of years ago that we have seen fulfilled in our lifetime.

For a list of prophecies fulfilled since AD 1948, see Appendix A.

Now let's look at the Gnostic books and see why the ancient church rejected them.

Books of the Gnostics

What we know about the Gnostics came mainly from the church fathers Irenaeus and Hippolytus until the discovery of a Gnostic library in Nag Hammadi, Egypt, in 1945. The contents of this library confirm what the church fathers stated had been the current Gnostic belief system.

There is an ancient fragment from the early church called the Muratorian Canon Fragment. It is named after the man who discovered it. It is missing the first section that refers to Matthew and Mark, and ends abruptly, but it gives a few details on which heretics and their books were rejected. We will see that these are some of the same Gnostic works found at Nag Hammadi.

The English translation of the fragment is as follows:

Matthew and Mark
...at which nevertheless he was present and so he placed it in his narrative.

Luke
The third book of the gospel is that according to Luke. Luke, the well-known physician, wrote it in his own name, according to the general belief after the ascension of Christ when Paul had associated him with himself as one zealous for correctness, one who took pains to find out the facts. It is true that he had

not seen the Lord in the flesh. Yet having ascertained the facts, he was able to begin his narrative with the nativity of John.

John

The fourth book of the gospel is that of John's, one of the disciples. In response to the exhortation of his fellow disciples and bishops he said, "Fast with me for three days, then let us tell each other whatever shall be revealed to each one." The same night it was revealed to Andrew, who was one of the apostles, that it was John who should relate in his own name what they collectively remembered; or that John was to relate in his own name, they all acting as correctors. And so to the faith of believers there is no discord even although different selections are given from the facts in the individual books of the Gospels. Because in all of them under the one guiding Spirit, all the things relative to His nativity, passion, resurrection, conversation with His disciples, and His twofold advent, the first in humiliation rising from contempt which took place; and the second, in the glory of kingly power which is yet to come, have been declared. What marvel it is then if John induces so consistently in his epistles these several things saying in person, "what we have seen with our eyes and heard with our ears and our hands have handled, those things we have written." For thus he professes to be not only an eyewitness, but also a hearer and a narrator of all the wonderful things of the Lord in their order.

Acts

Moreover the acts of all the apostles are written in one book. Luke so comprised them for the most excellent Theophilus because of the individual events that took place in his presence, as he clearly shows by omitting the passion of Peter, as well as the departure of Paul, when Paul went from the city of Rome to Spain. Now, the epistles of Paul, what they are and for what reason they were sent, they themselves make clear to him who will understand.

Paul

First of all he wrote at length to the Corinthians to prohibit the system of heresy, then to the Galatians against circumcision. And to the Romans on the order of Scriptures intimating also that Christ is the chief matter in them. Each of which is necessary for us to discuss seeing that the blessed apostle Paul himself, following the example of his predecessor John, writes to no more than seven churches by name, in the following order: Corinthians, Ephesians, Philippians, Colossians, Galatians, Thessalonians, and Romans. But he writes twice for the sake of correction to the Corinthians and to the Thessalonians.

Forgeries

That there is one church defused throughout the whole earth is shown, by this seven-fold writing and John also in the Apocalypse. Even though he writes to the seven churches, he speaks to all. But he wrote out of affection and love, one to Philemon, one to Titus, two to Timothy and these are held sacred in the honorable esteem of the church universal, in the regulation of Ecclesiastical discipline. There are adduced one to the Laodiceans, another to the Alexandrians, forged in the name of Paul against the heresy of Marcion. And many others which can't be received into the church universal, for it is not fitting that gall be mixed with honey.

General Epistles
Further an epistle of Jude, and two bearing the name of John, are counted among the general epistles. And Wisdom written by the friends of Solomon in his honor. We receive the Apocalypses of John and Peter only. Some of us do not wish the Apocalypse of Peter to be read in church.

Non-Inspired
But Hermas wrote "the Shepherd" in the city of Rome most recently in our times, when his brother bishop Pious was occupying the chair in the church at Rome. And so indeed it ought to be read, but that it be made public to the people in the church and placed among the prophets whose number is complete or among the apostles, is not possible to the end of time.

Gnostic Cults
We reject everything written by Arsenus, Valentinus, or Miltiadees. We also reject those also who wrote the "new book of Psalms", Marcion, together with Basilides, and the Asian Cataphrigians...

Books of the Gnostics

The ancient church made it clear there were only four Gospels. Gospels other than Matthew Mark, Luke and John were fake works produced by cults.

"The Apostles did not pass down any hidden wisdom, just the Scriptures."
Irenaeus, *Against Heresies 3.3*

"The doctrine of the apostles has been guarded and preserved without any forging of Scriptures, as a very complete system of doctrine. Neither receive addition to, nor suffer curtailment from, its truths. Read the Word of God without falsification, lawfully and diligently explaining the Old Testament in harmony with the rest of the Scriptures." Irenaeus, *Against Heresies 4.33*

"There never was any secret doctrine handed down by the apostles, just the Scriptures. Only the heretics say there is a secret doctrine from the apostles which you must know to correctly understand the Scripture."
Clement of Alexandria, *Stromata Book 2.4*

"The apostles did not keep any secret doctrine, but taught it all openly. Only heretics teach a secret gospel or letter or teaching."
Tertullian, *Prescription Against Heretics 1.25*

Demonic Gospels

> "The apostles did not give special information to favorite friends."
> Tertullian, *Prescription Against Heretics 1.26*

Here is a list of the books found at Nag Hammadi. The finding of these books proves that the church fathers were right all along.

The Nag Hammadi texts (pure Gnostic works)
1. Acts of Peter and the Twelve Apostles
2. Allogenes
3. Apocalypse of Adam
4. (First) Apocalypse of James
5. (Second) Apocalypse of James
6. Apocalypse of Paul
7. Apocalypse of Peter
8. Apocryphon of James
9. Apocryphon of John
10. Asclepius 21-29
11. Authoritative Teaching
12. Book of Thomas the Contender
13. Concept of Our Great Power
14. Dialogue of the Savior
15. Discourse on the Eighth and Ninth
16. Eugnostos the Blessed
17. Exegesis on the Soul
18. Gospel of the Egyptians
19. Gospel of Philip
20. Gospel of Thomas
21. Gospel of Truth
22. Hypostasis of the Archons

23. Hypsiphrone
24. Interpretation of Knowledge
25. Letter of Peter to Philip
26. Marsanes
27. Melchizedek
28. On the Anointing
29. On the Baptism A
30. On the Baptism B
31. On the Eucharist A
32. On the Eucharist B
33. On the Origin of the World
34. Paraphrase of Shem
35. Plato, Republic 588A-589B
36. Prayer of the Apostle Paul
37. Prayer of Thanksgiving
38. Second Treatise of the Great Seth
39. Sentences of Sextus
40. Sophia of Jesus Christ
41. Teachings of Silvanus
42. Testimony of Truth
43. Thought of Norea
44. Three Steles of Seth
45. Thunder, Perfect Mind
46. Treatise on the Resurrection
47. Trimorphic Protennoia
48. Tripartite Tractate
49. A Valentinian Exposition
50. Zostrianos

Fake Gospels
1. Assumption of the Virgin

Demonic Gospels
2. Birth of Mary
3. Gospel of Barnabas (Arabic)
4. Gospel of Bartholomew
5. Gospel of Basilides
6. Gospel of Ebionites
7. Gospel of the Hebrews
8. Gospel of Marcion
9. Gospel of Matthias
10. Gospel of Nicodemus
11. Gospel of Pseudo-Matthew
12. Gospel of Thomas (Infancy)
13. History of Joseph the Carpenter
14. Infancy Gospel (Arabic)
15. Infancy Gospel (Armenian)
16. Protevanglium of James
17. Resurrection of Christ by Bartholomew

Fake Acts and Epistles
1. Acts of Abodias
2. Acts of Andrew
3. Acts of Andrew (fragment)
4. Acts of Andrew and Matthais
5. Acts of Barnabas
6. Acts of James, Ascents
7. Acts of James the Great
8. Acts of John
9. Acts of John, by Prochorus
10. Acts of Paul
11. Acts of Peter
12. Acts of Peter (Slavonic)
13. Acts of Peter and Andrew

14. Acts of Peter and Paul
15. Acts of Philip
16. Acts of Pilate
17. Acts of Thaddeus
18. Acts of Thomas
19. Matthew, Martyrdom of
20. Paul and Seneca
21. Paul and Thecla
22. Peter, Preaching of
23. Peter, Passion of
24. Peter and Paul, Passion of
25. Epistle of Titus (not to be confused with the biblical Epistle of Titus)

Fake Apocalypses
1. Apocalypse of the Virgin
2. Apocalypse of Paul
3. Apocalypse of Ezra (Greek)
4. Apocalypse of Adam (Gnostic)
5. Apocalypse of Abraham
6. Apocalypse of Daniel
7. Elchasai, Book of
8. Naassene Psalm

Miscellaneous
1. Life of Adam and Eve
2. First book of Adam and Eve
3. Second book of Adam and Eve
4. Second Enoch
5. Third Enoch
6. Secrets of Enoch

Demonic Gospels

7. Second Baruch
8. Third Baruch
9. Fourth Baruch
10. Testament of Adam
11. Testament of Abraham
12. Testament of Isaac
13. Testament of Jacob
14. Testament of Solomon
15. Ladder of Jacob
16. History of the Rechabites
17. History of Joseph
18. Ezekiel Apocryphon
19. Treefold Fruits
20. Good Tidings of Seth

Gnostic Belief

The Gnostics were the cults of the first century. Starting with Simon Magus, who is called the father of Gnosticism, Gnosticism fragmented into as many as twenty-two different groups. Each of these groups had a few unique teachings but the basic doctrine was still the same. Gnostic belief included the following:

There are thirty aeons (gods) that exist in the Pleroma, outside time and space.[a] The goddess, Sophia, created the demiurge, a creator angel (the God of the Old Testament) who was a tyrant; and being unaware of the aeons, thought he was the only God. He created man; but Sophia gave man a spirit.[b] Some may be saved if they do enough good works; but some are predestined to go to hell.[c] Gnostics have spirits that are emanations from Sophia. This makes them predestined to be saved. It is impossible for them to lose their salvation. It does not matter if their behavior is good or evil. The most "perfect" of them addict themselves to evil deeds and are in the habit of defiling the women they convert.[d] Eventually all matter will be destroyed, since matter is evil and not capable of salvation.[e] They utter mantras to effect nature.[f] The

---

[a] Irenaeus, *Against Heresies* 1.1-3
[b] Irenaeus, *Against Heresies* 1.5
[c] Irenaeus, *Against Heresies* 1.7; 4.37
[d] Irenaeus, *Against Heresies* 1.6
[e] Irenaeus, *Against Heresies* 1.7, 23
[f] Irenaeus, *Against Heresies* 1.14-15

Demonic Gospels

demiurge created Adam and Eve and enslaved them. Sophia sent a creator angel in the form of a serpent into the Garden of Eden to free Eve and Adam. By eating from the tree they attained true gnosis and were set free.[g] Sophia saved Noah from the flood sent by the evil demiurge.

Let's look at some of the peculiar doctrines of the major Gnostic cults.

Simon Magus
Simon Magus was the father of the Gnostic movement. He had a counterfeit faith and used exorcisms and incantations, love-potions, and charms, as well as those beings who are called "Paredri" (familiars) and "Oniropompi" (dream-senders).[h] He allegorized much Scripture to support his teachings,[i] especially Genesis.

Menander
Menander was a disciple of Simon Magus. When he broke away and formed his own Gnostic cult he taught that by means of magic one may overcome the angels that made the world. Only if you were baptized into Menander would you obtain resurrection and never die, again having eternal youth.[j]

---

[g] Irenaeus, *Against Heresies* 1.30
[h] Irenaeus, *Against Heresies* 1.23
[i] Hippolytus, *Heresies* 6.5-10
[j] Irenaeus, *Against Heresies* 1.23

Gnostic Belief

Nicolaitans
The Nicolaitans practiced adultery, and ate things sacrificed to idols.[k] In the course of time they became very obscene.[l]

Carpocrates
Carpocrates was a magician and a fornicator.[m] He practiced magical arts, incantations, spells, and held voluptuous feasts. His followers were in the habit of invoking the aid of subordinate demons and dream-senders.[n] He taught that humans are imprisoned in a cycle of reincarnation by those evil creator angels, but would eventually break the cycle and be saved,[o] and he said Nicolas and Mathias taught fornication is no longer wrong.[p]

Saturninus
Saturninus said he, himself, was an angel; Jesus did not have a physical body; Jesus came to destroy the god of the Jews; and sex, marriage, and reproduction are sinful.[q] Saturnilus and his school were vegetarians. Marriage and procreation were said to be instituted by Satan and they practiced asceticism.[r]

Marcus
Marcus taught that the Holy Spirit put a drop of her blood into the wine when he blessed it. Upon drinking it,

---

[k] Irenaeus, *Against Heresies* 1.26; 5.1
[l] Tertullian, *Heresies* 1.1
[m] Tertullian, *Treatise of the Soul* 1.35
[n] Hippolytus, *Heresies* 7.20
[o] Irenaeus, *Against Heresies* 1.25
[p] Clement of Alexandria, *Stromata* 3.4
[q] Irenaeus, *Against Heresies* 1.24, 28
[r] Hippolytus, *Heresies* 7.16

Demonic Gospels

followers would understand mysteries and prophesy.[s] This was the beginning of the false doctrine of transubstantiation. Marcus said the cup imparted grace if he used a special incantation.[t] Marcus taught a second baptism [of redemption] by the laying on of hands. Marcus also gave a word or phrase [Mantra] when he decided the follower was ready to go on to the higher mysteries, or when the disciple was dying [last rites]. They were taught to keep secret the word and even deny that it existed.[u]

Marcion

Marcion rejected the Old Testament and used cut up versions of Luke and some of Paul's epistles. He taught the God of the Old Testament and His prophets were evil and would be destroyed.[v] He taught God is the author of sin;[w] there were two equal and opposite gods, one good and one evil;[x] and that the Law and the Gospel being so against each other proved two different gods.[y] He was strongly addicted to astrology,[z] taught there was no resurrection and that the saved should not marry. [aa] He removed references in his gospel to Christ as creator, [bb] and said Jesus was a phantom [did not have a physical body]. [cc]

---

[s] Irenaeus, *Against Heresies* 1.13
[t] Hippolytus, *Heresies* 6.34-35
[u] Hippolytus, *Heresies* 6.36-37
[v] Irenaeus, *Against Heresies* 1.27
[w] Clement of Alexandria, *Against Heresies* 4.29
[x] Tertullian, *Against Marcion* 1.2
[y] Tertullian, *Against Marcion* 1.19-20
[z] Tertullian, *Against Marcion* 1.18
[aa] Tertullian, *Against Marcion* 1.24
[bb] Tertullian, *Against Marcion* 2.17
[cc] Tertullian, *Against Marcion* 3.8, 4.8

Gnostic Belief

Titian
Titian said Adam was not saved,[dd] drinking wine was a sin,[ee] and that the soul was not eternal; it dissolved with the body [soul sleep].[ff] He also taught medicine was demonic, and instead of taking it, we should rely on God alone. [gg]

Elchasaites
The Elchasaites taught Jesus incarnated many times. They resorted to incantations and baptisms in their confession of elements. They occupied themselves with bustling activity in regard to astrological and mathematical science, and of the arts of sorcery. But they also alleged themselves to have powers of precognition.[hh]

Naasseni
Naasseni worshiped the serpent; taught their order was started by James, the Lord's brother, and that Adam was a hermaphrodite. They used the *Gospel According to Thomas*, some things taken from the Mysteries of Isis, and Mysteries of the Assyrians, and they practiced orgies.[ii]

Peratae
The Peratae taught a kind of tri-theism.[jj] Another branch of the Peratae taught Jesus was the Son of the serpent.[kk]

[dd] Irenaeus, *Against Heresies* 3.23
[ee] Clement of Alexandria, *Instructor* 2.2
[ff] Titian, *Greeks* 13
[gg] Titian, *Greeks* 18
[hh] Hippolytus, *Heresies* 10.25
[ii] Hippolytus, *Heresies* 5.1
[jj] Hippolytus, *Heresies* 5.7
[kk] Hippolytus, *Heresies* 5.12

Demonic Gospels

Basilides

Basilides taught reincarnation with karma, man could grow up and be sinless all of his life,[ll] [born without original sin] and that spirits [sometimes animal spirits] latched on to mankind and forced them to sin. He taught saving faith was intellectual ascent. All humans were born with this ability [Pelegianism].[mm] After baptism God forgave involuntary sins but sinners had to pay for all voluntary sins in order to be purged from them [penance, purgatory, cardinal and venial sins].[nn] He also taught that Jesus was transformed to look like Simon of Cyrene, and that Simon was crucified in His place.[oo] He taught the name of the most supreme god was Abraxas.[pp] This is where we get the magic word "Abracadabra."

Valentinus

Valentinus said saving faith came from your spirit, if you were one of the chosen [men are born saved],[qq] and some were not predestined to be saved, but were predestined for hell, but the rest might be saved through works.[rr] Only those whose spirit was an emanation from Sophia were predestined to be saved. All others were predestined to hell [double predestination],[ss] and those predestined for salvation did not need to practice good works.[tt]

[ll] Clement of Alexandria, *Stromata* 4.12
[mm] Clement of Alexandria, *Stromata* 2.3,20; 4.13
[nn] Clement of Alexandria, *Stromata* 4.24
[oo] Irenaeus, *Against Heresies* 1.24; Tertullian, *Heresies* 1.1
[pp] Tertullian, *Heresies* 1.1
[qq] Clement of Alexandria, *Stromata* 2.3,20; 4.13
[rr] Tertullian, *Valentians* 1.29
[ss] Clement of Alexandria, *Stromata* 2.3,20; 4.13
[tt] Tertullian, *Valentians* 1.30

Gnostic Belief

The ancient church made it clear that a person could not believe Gnosticism and still be a true Christian.

> "When they are called Phrygians, Novatians, Valentinians, Marcionites, Anthropians, or Arians, they have ceased to be Christians."
> Lactantius, *Divine Institutes 4.30*

Truth vs. Demonic Doctrine

We now know that the Scriptures were put together by prophets who proved themselves to be inspired by God through fulfilled prophecy. Since the Gnostic gospels do not have any verifiable, recently fulfilled prophecy to back them up like the Bible has, we must look at the basic teachings of the Gospel from the Bible and then contrast that with the teachings of the Gnostic gospels to see the problems with them. The main points of the true gospel we need to look at are:

1. There is, and always will be, only one God.
2. We are not gods, nor are we evolving into gods.
3. Salvation is based on Christ's work, not our works.
4. The use of meditation and idolatry is wrong.
5. We resurrect, we do not reincarnate.

Let's look at these in detail:

There is and always will be only one God
There are not two or more separate gods or goddesses. The Scriptures clearly teach there is only *one* God.

> "Ye *are* my witnesses, saith the LORD, and my Servant whom I have chosen: that ye may know and believe Me, and understand that I *am* He: before Me there was no God formed, neither shall there be after Me." *Isaiah 43:10*

I *am* the LORD, and *there is* none else, *there is* no God beside Me: I girded thee, though thou hast not known Me: that they may know from the rising of the sun, and from the west, that *there is* none beside Me. I *am* the LORD, and *there is* none else.
Isaiah 45:5-6

"Look unto Me, and be ye saved, all the ends of the earth: for I *am* God, and *there is* none else."
Isaiah 45:22

"Fear ye not, neither be afraid: have not I told thee from that time, and have declared *it?* Ye *are* even My witnesses. Is there a God beside me? Yea, *there is* no God; I know not *any.*" *Isaiah 44:8*

"As concerning therefore the eating of those things that are offered in sacrifice unto idols, we know that an idol *is* nothing in the world, and that *there is* none other God but one." *1 Corinthians 8:4*

We are not evolving into gods.

Satan thought he was evolving into a god who would surpass the Creator of the universe. He was wrong.

"How art thou fallen from heaven, O Lucifer, son of the morning! *how* art thou cut down to the ground, which didst weaken the nations! For thou hast said in thine heart, I will ascend into heaven, I will exalt my throne above the stars of God: I will sit also upon the mount of the congregation, in the sides of

Demonic Gospels

> the north: I will ascend above the heights of the clouds; I will be like the most High. Yet thou shalt be brought down to hell, to the sides of the pit."
> *Isaiah 14:12-15*

> "Adam was saved, contrary to Tatian. There was no way possible for Adam to become a god."
> Irenaeus, *Against Heresies 3.23*

Salvation is based on Christ's work, not our works
Scriptures clearly teach that salvation is based on what Jesus did on the cross. We must trust Him for salvation. We do not meditate or evolve into gods in order to obtain salvation. There is absolutely nothing we can do about our salvation other than to accept it as a free gift; it is all up to Jesus Christ.

> "That if thou shalt confess with thy mouth the Lord Jesus, and shalt believe in thine heart that God hath raised him from the dead, thou shalt be saved. For with the heart man believeth unto righteousness; and with the mouth confession is made unto salvation."
> *Romans 10:9-10*

> "For by grace are ye saved through faith; and that not of yourselves: *it is* the gift of God: Not of works, lest any man should boast." *Ephesians 2:8-9*

The use of Meditation and idolatry is wrong
We do not meditate, use idols, or make ourselves into idols by declaring our own godhood. These things are sin.

"Thou shalt have no other gods before me. Thou shalt not make unto thee any graven image, or any likeness *of anything* that *is* in heaven above, or that *is* in the earth beneath, or that *is* in the water under the earth: Thou shalt not bow down thyself to them, nor serve them: for I the LORD thy God *am* a jealous God, visiting the iniquity of the fathers upon the children unto the third and fourth *generation* of them that hate me; and shewing mercy unto thousands of them that love me, and keep my commandments."
Exodus 20:3-6

"There shall not be found among you *any one* that maketh his son or his daughter to pass through the fire, *or* that useth divination, *or* an observer of times, or an enchanter, or a witch, or a charmer, or a consulter with familiar spirits, or a wizard, or a necromancer. For all that do these things *are* an abomination unto the LORD: and because of these abominations the LORD thy God doth drive them out from before thee." *Deuteronomy 18:10-12*

"The spirits speaking through the pagan prophets claim to be God, but their speech is "strange, fanatical, and quite unintelligible words, of which no rational person can find the meaning: for so dark are they, as to have no meaning at all; but they give occasion to every fool or impostor to apply them to suit his own purposes." Origen, *Against Celsus 7:9*

"True prophets speak the plain truth and sometimes in parables and enigmas, but spiritual Christians can always figure out the riddles. Satan will counterfeit with riddles that have no real meaning."
Origen, *Against Celsus 7:10*

"The church does not perform anything by means of angelic invocations, or incantations, or by any other wicked curious art; but, directing her prayers to the Lord." Irenaeus, *Against Heresies 2.32*

"[Heretics] hear alike, and pray alike – even with pagans."
Tertullian, *Prescription Against Heretics 42*

"They [Christians] cannot tolerate temples, altars, or images." Origen, *Against Celsus 7.42*

"A true prophet under the control of the Holy Spirit does not fall into ecstasy or madness like the pagans do." Origen, *Against Celsus 7:3*

We resurrect, we do not reincarnate

Everyone, both the saved and the unsaved, will physically resurrect. We have Jesus as our example. Paul makes it clear that there will be a physical resurrection.

"Moreover, brethren, I declare unto you the gospel which I preached unto you, which also ye have received, and wherein ye stand; by which also ye are saved, if ye keep in memory what I preached unto you, unless ye have believed in vain. For I delivered unto you first of all that which I also received, how that Christ died for our sins according to the scriptures; and that He was buried, and that He rose again the third day according to the Scriptures: and that He was seen of Cephas, then of the twelve: after that, He was seen of above five hundred brethren at once; of whom the greater part remain unto this present, but some are fallen asleep. After that, He was seen of James; then of all the apostles. And last of all He was seen of me also, as of one born out of due time." *1 Corinthians 15:1-8*

Paul states that in order to be a Christian one must believe in the physical resurrection. This means Christians deny the doctrine of reincarnation. Resurrection and reincarnation cannot both be true.

"Now if Christ be preached that He rose from the dead, how say some among you that there is no resurrection of the dead? But if there be no resurrection of the dead, then is Christ not risen: and if Christ be not risen, then *is* our preaching vain, and your faith *is* also vain. Yea, and we are found false witnesses of God; because we have testified of God that He raised up Christ: whom He raised not up, if so be that the dead rise not. For if the dead rise not, then is not Christ raised: and if Christ be not raised, your faith *is* vain; ye are yet in your sins. Then they also which are fallen asleep in Christ are perished."
1 Corinthians 15:12-18

Demonic Gospels

Conclusion

The Bible proves itself by prophecy, teaches salvation is by Christ's work alone, and teaches there is only one God. The Scriptures teach that eastern style meditation, or sorcery, and idolatry are wrong, and that we will all physically resurrect.

Any ancient document that teaches multiple gods, creator angels, creator spirits, or that we are evolving into gods is demonic. Any ancient document that teaches we should use idols, sorcery, or meditation is demonic. And finally, any ancient document that teaches we can save ourselves by works, meditation, enlightenment, or something else, is clearly demonic!

This being said, we will show that the Gnostic gospels teach these demonic doctrines and, therefore, are not of God, but a trick of Satan to lead us astray and into hell.

They are demonic gospels!

Gnostic Gospels

Gospel of Barnabas

The *Gospel of Barnabas* is a fake work. The English version was translated in the early 1900's from the Italian version. The Italian translation could be as old as 1400 AD. No other copies exist, and there are no references to it from anyone before the 1500's AD.

The Gospel of Barnabas should not be confused with the *Epistle of Barnabas,* which dates between 70 and 135 AD. The epistle may, or may not, have been written by the Barnabas of Acts, but it is quoted by early church fathers like Clement of Alexandria, who stated about 170 AD, the epistle was authentic. The teachings in the *Epistle of Barnabas* agree completely with the Bible.

Many times Muslims will cite this fake *Gospel of Barnabas* in order to try to prove the Bible has been tampered with and the Quran is correct. Most of them do not realize that it contradicts both the Bible and the Quran in many places. Knowing this may help in witnessing to Muslims.

The *Gospel of Barnabas* says Jesus stated, "I am not the Messiah" (sec. 42, 48) which contradicts both the Bible (Matthew 16) and Quran (sura 5). It calls Paul apostate, and says circumcision is necessary for salvation (Sec. 23). Other statements that contradict the Bible include: Jesus did not die on the cross; Judas died in His place

(Sec 217); and Jesus is not God incarnate. It contradicts both the biblical gospels and history by saying that "Jesus was born when Pilate was governor" (Sec 3). It says "Jesus sailed to Nazareth" which of course has no seaport (Sec 20). It says Mary brought forth her son without pain (Sec 3), which contradicts the Quran in sura 19:23.

The Quran condemns eating pork, but the *Gospel of Barnabas* says "that which enters into the man does not defile the man, but that which comes out of the man defiles the man" (32).

It says Daniel was taken captive by Nebuchadnezzar when he was two years old (Sec. 80), which contradicts Daniel 1:1.

It does, however, teach the wise men worshiped Jesus (Sec. 6) which agrees with the Bible, but contradicts the Quran.

Gospel of the Egyptians

This seems to be a mixture of common Egyptian elements (the Ogdoad) and Sethian Gnosticism. This Gnostic gospel teaches that in the beginning there existed only the "Unknowable Father." He created three powers called the Father, the Mother, and the Son. When the three powers are separated, they reveal eight qualities each. These three powers are called the Barbelo. The Unknowable Father also brought forth eight beings from the silence of his mind. These were called the Ogdoad, and they created the æons. The Apocryphon of John, also called the Secret book of John, also describes the first cause as the "Unknowable Father."

The Unknowable Father, or evolving first parent, emanated a being called "Christ." The Christ emanated the first human being called Adamas. Something terrible happened. We are not told much about what happened except it was an attack by an æon named Sakla, accompanied by a demon named Nebruel. Adamas moved to correct "the deficiency." He emanated a divine son named Seth.

All of Seth's descendants contain the divine in them. Seth sent four hundred angels to protect his children. Later, he incarnated as Jesus Christ. He did not come to die on a cross to pay for our sins; but instead, to teach us the path to discover our own unique incorruptibility.

Gospel of Egyptians

According to this false gospel, the path to knowledge, or salvation, comes by five seals of Gnosis. The first seal, or sacrament, is water baptism. Along the path of these five seals one is awakened and begins to see visions and speak in diverse languages. A sample of the babbling that begins the "voices" stage of the rites is given in the text.

IE IEUS EO OU EO OUA!
O Yesseus Mazareus Yessedekeus,
O living water, O child of the child, O glorious name!
AION O ON,
IIII EEEE EEEE OOOO UUUU OOOO AAAA
EI AAAA OOOO, O
Existing one who sees the Aeons!
A EEEEE IIII UUUUUU OOOOOOOO,
Who is eternally eternal!
IEA AIO,
In the heart, who exists
U AEI EIS AEI
EI O EI, EI OS EI
You are what you are
SOU IES IDE AEIO OIS,
O AEON, AEON,
O God of Silence!

If correctly done, the "voices" stage would bring about a meditative silence that would initiate an experience of transcendence. This would begin to open up one's divine spark.

Demonic Gospels

This texts ends by stating it was written by the great Seth during the 120 years before the great Flood. To ensure that the demiurge did not destroy all traces of the truth in this coming Flood, the great Seth placed copies of this text in secret underground chambers in the two cities where these rites have always been performed. Modern readers would know these two cites as Sodom and Gomorrah!

"The *Gospel of the Hebrews*...and the *Gospel of the Egyptians* are disputed by most.
Clement of Alexandria, *Stromata 3.10*

Gospel of Judas

The Canites were an ancient Gnostic sect that taught Cain, Judas, the sodomites, Esau, Korah, and other ungodly persons were true enlightened men who fought against the evil creator god. They produced the famous *Gospel of Judas*, which is full of Gnostic ideas. In *Against Heresies 1.2*, Tertullian taught the Cainites worshiped Cain as the incarnation of the supreme pure god and despised the Creator God of the Old Testament as an inferior god.

The *Gospel of Judas* teaches that Jesus came to destroy the works of the God of the Old Testament. Judas and Jesus secretly entered into a pact that would cause the crucifixion and thereby destroy man's enslavement to the God of the Old Testament. Once freed, men could become gods.

According to the *Gospel of Judas*, Jesus told Judas that the disciples were mortal and would never see heaven, and that most humans were predestined for eternal damnation. But he [Judas] had a soul from the great Seth and was therefore immortal. He would live eternally with the angels, æons, and the creator mother (Holy Spirit). Further, those who are of the seed of Seth would find their way into gnosis which would lead them into transcendence.

Demonic Gospels

> "The Gnostic sect of Cainites... maintain that Judas the traitor was thoroughly acquainted with these things. They even produced a fictitious history of this kind, which they call the Gospel of Judas." Irenaeus, *Against Heresies 1.31.1*

In contrast, the Bible states that Judas was the one who betrayed Jesus for thirty pieces of silver (which was a fulfilled prophecy from Zechariah 13:6-7). The biblical gospel of John (13:27) says Satan entered him, and the betrayal of Jesus was so evil that Judas would never be forgiven (John 17:12).

Gospel of Mary

There are three surviving manuscripts of this work. The oldest is written in Sahidic Coptic. The other two are in Greek. Only a portion remains of the entire gospel. It does not say which Mary is present; but based on the doctrines of the ancient Gnostics, it would be Mary Magdalene.

The existent part of this gospel begins with the disciples questioning Jesus. Most of questions seem nonsensical. After talking about the destruction of matter, Jesus is asked: what is the sin of the world? Jesus answered that there is no such thing as real sin. Sin is only sin if you want it to be.

Later, after Jesus had departed, Peter asked Mary to share with them something that Jesus had taught her secretly. She shared how to see Jesus in visions, not by the spirit, or soul, but by using the power of her mind. To do this one must be able to ascend up through the seven powers: darkness, desire, ignorance, death desire, flesh desire, foolish fleshly wisdom, and wrathful wisdom. Then you can arrive at the realm of the silence of the mind.

Peter and Andrew reject this as heresy. Then Levi stands up for her, reminding the others that Jesus loved her more than all of them, so she would know the truth.

Demonic Gospels

We can see in this text the practice of contemplative prayer achieving the silence of the mind. One does not have to repent of sin, but simply acknowledge that there is no sin and contemplate the god spark within them.

Gnostics called Mary Magdalene "the apostle of apostles" and "the thirteenth apostle." They believed she was the true heir to Jesus' ministry. Peter could never quite understand and achieve true gnosis and neither did Rome. However, Mary Magdalene led the Gnostics into freedom (or salvation), not by Jesus' death on the cross, but by following His teaching. The Gnostics believed that Jesus taught that mediation or contemplative prayer was the path to God and ultimately salvation.

Some Gnostics also believed Mary Magdalene was the wife of Jesus. Some also thought there was a royal blood line down through the ages that began with the child of Mary and Jesus. Dan Brown's bestselling novel, *The Da Vinci Code,* was based on this Gnostic teaching.

Gospel of Philip

The Gnostic Gospel of Philip is another collection of supposed sayings of Jesus; but there is also a section on the Gnostic sacraments. The ancient church believed in two ordnances: baptism, and the Lord's Supper. The church taught these were rituals one did to show they understood what Christ had done for them. The ancient church did not believe they were anything more than a memorial. They did not impart grace or cause anything to happen. This gospel teaches there were five Gnostic sacraments: baptism, chrism (anointing with oil), redemption, bridal chamber, and the Eucharist.

According to the Gospel of Philip, the first sacrament of water baptism erases original sin and begins the process of entering into the spiritual realm. The second sacrament, chrism, where one is anointed with oil, is called a "baptism of light." This is where a Gnostic received the feminine Holy Spirit.

The sacrament of redemption is where one is initiated into sorcery, or Gnostic meditation. The description is very similar to the modern initiation rite of Transcendental Meditation.

> "Marcus taught a baptism of redemption, by a laying on of hands. He would give a word or phrase [mantra] when he decides the follower is

ready to go on to the higher mysteries, or when the disciple is dying [last rites]. They are taught to keep secret the word and even deny that it exists."
Hippolytus, *Heresies 6.36-37*

The fourth sacrament is that of the bridal chamber. It was important that a male and female Gnostic undergo the rite of the bridal chamber because it connected the two in such a spiritual way that could not be achieved by one person alone. All we know about it is that the church fathers taught it was connected with fornication and astrology. This sounds like the tantric sex magic of the Hindus. This is what church father Irenaeus taught:

> "Gnostics believe they have spirits that are emanations from Sophia. This makes them predestined to be saved. It does not matter if their behavior is good or evil. The most "perfect" of them addict themselves to evil deeds and are in a habit of defiling the women they convert.
> Irenaeus, *Against Heresies 1.6*

The *Gospel of Philip* seems to indicate that the sacrament of the bridal chamber is the most important for attaining godhood. The sacrament of the bridal chamber is also mentioned in the *Gospel of Thomas*, saying 75. It must be entered into by a free man and virgin. Defiled women, slaves, and animals could not partake of the rite.

The gospel also teaches that there are "sons of men who create." Those are the ones whose children are ensnared

Gospel of Philip

by the world and its evil; they are normal human beings. There are also "sons of men who beget." These beget in private (the bridal chamber) and their offspring are the "sons of light." It also states those who have received the light of the bridal chamber are free since they cannot be seen by evil.

It has been suggested, based on this gospel and what the ancient church fathers indicated, that a sexual union between a man and woman in a controlled manner with the necessary magical incantations would allow spiritual development of the individuals. Going a step further, it would allow a child born from that union to have a spirit that is an emanation from Sophia and therefore immortal. The church fathers saw this as an excuse for the Gnostics to defile any woman they chose.

> "A horse sires a horse, a man begets man, a god brings forth a god." *Gospel of Philip*

We see this same idea in occult circles today.

Jesus and Mary Magdalene

The *Gospel of Philip* suggests that Jesus' love for Mary Magdalene was more than disciple and master, but husband and wife. It says Jesus loved Mary more than the other disciples. It calls Mary the companion and consort of Jesus and states that "Jesus kissed her often on the…" The next word is missing, being smudged out.

Mary, an Ever Virgin

The *Gospel of Philip* also denies Mary, the mother of Jesus, conceived Him by the Holy Spirit. They believed the Holy Spirit is female, so how could a female conceive with another female?

> "Some said, 'Mary conceived by the Holy Spirit.' They are in error. They do not know what they are saying. When did a woman ever conceive by a woman? Mary is the virgin whom no power ever defiled." *Gospel of Philip*

Gospel of Pseduo-Matthew

This Gnostic work begins by stating that Anna became pregnant by a miracle when an angel came to her. She had not seen her husband in over twenty years. By the time her child Mary was three years old, Mary could walk and talk and take care of herself like a thirty-year-old. She married Joseph who was old and had grown children of his own. She remained a virgin all of her life. Lions, panthers, and dragons came and worshiped Jesus in Bethlehem. The child Jesus did many miracles, and even killed a boy with His powers who was making fun of Him. Later a teacher tried to make Jesus say His alphabet and Jesus became angry. The teacher dropped dead. These stories are almost identical with the ones in the *Infancy Gospels*.

> "It [Pseudo-Matthew] was published by a disciple cf Manichæus named Leucius, who also wrote the falsely styled Acts of the Apostles."
> *Jerome's Letter to Bishop Cromatius*

Gospel of Thomas

The Gnostic *Gospel of Thomas* is written in Egyptian Coptic and dated from about AD 340. There exist also earlier Greek versions. See *Infancy Gospels* for details. It is not a narration of the life of Jesus Christ, but a collection of His supposed sayings. Some of these one hundred and fourteen sayings are nearly identical with the ones found in the New Testament Gospels. Other sayings are completely different. A few of the sayings are also found in the *Gospel of the Hebrews* and *Egyptians*, but some are not found anywhere else.

It does not give any interpretations for the sayings or parables found in the text. Some of the sayings lead to a belief in dualism (that there are two opposite and equal gods; one good, and the other bad).

The reason why the history was stripped away and just the sayings were left is because of the idea of gnosis. The sayings are not in any particular order, but randomized for the purpose of meditation.

The book itself states that the way to gain eternal life is by stripping away everything worldly from your life and sequestering yourself away in a lifestyle of Gnostic mediation. If you focus on the sayings during mediation, or contemplative prayer, it will open you up to a higher

Gospel of Thomas

plane of existence. The sayings are what it takes to make you realize you are a christ.

Some of the teachings contained in this gospel are:
1. People have an essence of God in them.
2. Salvation is finding the light within oneself.
3. Women are only saved if they make themselves spiritually male.
4. Adam came from a great power.

Some odd "quotes of Jesus" in this gospel are:
1. Whoever will drink from My mouth will become like Me.
2. Whoever will come to know father and mother, he will be called son of a whore.
3. I will destroy this house, and no one will be able to build it again.
4. His disciples said to Him: "When will the resurrection of the dead take place, and when will the new world come?" He said to them: "That resurrection which you are waiting for has already come, but you do not recognize it."
5. Where there are three gods, they are gods.
6. If you pray, you will be condemned.
7. If you fast, you are sinning.

We see many Gnostic heresies in these sayings. Adam was created not by the one true God, but a lesser power. There are multiple gods. There is no physical resurrection; it is a spiritual symbol of gaining godhood. Women are only saved if they become spiritually male.

Demonic Gospels

This is probably associated with the sacrament of sacred marriage. Women are inferior to men and must undergo the ritual to make them equal, only then can they begin the awakening unto true gnosis.

"The infancy *Gospel of Thomas* was the work of Gnostics and is a very wicked story."
Irenaeus, *Against Heresies 1.20*

"The Gnostic Naasseni use the *Gospel According to Thomas*."
Hippolytus, *Refutation of all Heresies 5.1*

Gospel of Truth

This gospel teaches that Jesus came from the Father, who dwells in the pleroma (Gnostic heaven beyond time and space), to destroy ignorance. People are ignorant because they have forgotten that they have a spark of the divine in them. The only way of rediscovering the Father is through the process of mystical experience.

True salvation is based on true repentance. True repentance is the process through gnosis (meditation) back to the knowledge of the divine.

There are three kinds of people in the world. The physics, who have a divine spark in them and are immortal. They will all eventually return to godhood. There are the pneumatics who have the possibility of becoming divine by good works and use of the proper rituals and incantations. Then there are the hyle. Hylic people are so sensual they have no chance of obtaining any form of salvation. These are predestined for eternal destruction.

One interesting thing about this gospel is that in addition to teaching how to awaken through gnosis (Gnostic meditation), it also has instruction on how to get through the nightmares. Apparently, at first, meditation causes nightmares. But in case one chose not to go through the process of nightmares, it gives the stern warning that

Demonic Gospels

gnosis is the only way of salvation, and unless you learn to meditate you *will* perish!

The *Gospel of Truth* describes the different kinds of nightmares followers will experience and why they are necessary to attaining the awakening. Once you have attained the awakening, separation from God is not possible.

In *Against Heresies 1.3.2* Irenaeus quotes passages of the *Gospel of Truth* stating it was a Valentinian work.

Hypostasis of the Archons and *On the Origin of the World* both contain references to Sophia's fall.

Infancy Gospels

There are two versions of the *Infancy Gospels* written in Greek, one in Latin, and what is called the *Gospel of Thomas*, written in Coptic. See the chapter on *Gospel of Thomas* for a discussion on that Gnostic work.

There are minor differences in the two Greek and the one Latin versions. Essentially, they report to be the events in Jesus' childhood. Some of these contradict biblical doctrine and are obviously fake. In the *Infancy Gospels*, the boy Jesus supposedly curses, kills people by divine power, and constantly seems to find ways of hurting people's feelings.

Greek Form 1
In chapter 3 of the first Greek form, the child Jesus becomes angry with a young boy and turns him into a wrinkled old man. In chapter 4, Jesus becomes angry with another boy and by His word alone, kills him. In chapter 5, Jesus makes people who did not like Him go blind. When Joseph reprimands Him, Jesus rebukes Joseph. In chapter 7, Jesus makes His teacher feel very foolish and ashamed. In chapter 8, Jesus maims people who spoke against Him. In chapter 9, Jesus raises a boy from the dead. In chapter 13, Jesus makes a piece of wood grow to fit in a plough Joseph was making. In chapter 14, Jesus kills his teacher because he hit Jesus in the head with a rod for smarting off to him. And in chapter 16, the child

Demonic Gospels

Jesus healed his older brother, James, from a snake bite and then makes the snake burst open and die.

Greek Form 2

The second Greek form is shorter. It leaves out some of the stories of the first Greek form, but chapter 2 is the same as the first Greek form's chapter 3, which teaches that Jesus becomes angry with a young boy and turns him into a wrinkled old man. Chapter 4 is the same as the first Greek form's chapter 4, teaching that Jesus becomes angry with another boy, and by His word alone, kills him. The other stories mentioned in Greek form 1 are omitted.

Latin Form

In chapter 1 of the Latin form, Jesus brings a fish back to life and makes it walk on water. In chapter 4, its gives the same story as chapter 4 of the two Greek forms, except Jesus calls the boy a sodomite, then kills him. It tells the story in chapter 5 that many parents come to Joseph in anger because Jesus had killed some of their children. The Latin chapter 12 is the same as the Greek chapter 14, and the Latin chapter 14 is the same as the Greek chapter 16.

"The infancy *Gospel of Thomas* was the work of Gnostics and is a very wicked story."
Irenaeus, *Against Heresies 1.20*

Protevangelium of James

The *Protevangelium of James* tells the story that Mary was born from Anna, who was barren. She gave Mary up to the temple (like Samuel). Upon entering the temple, Mary was given food from the hand of an angel. It teaches the following unbiblical ideas: Jesus was not born in Bethlehem and that Jesus was not born in the normal way, but just appeared. Church father Origen testified that it was a work of Gnostic heretics and that they wanted to teach the perpetual virginity of Mary because they wished her to be worshiped as one of their goddesses.

Chapter nine says that when Mary was twelve years old, the priests assembled and prayed to find out who could take Mary before she defiled the temple by coming into puberty. The men cast their rods down and prayed. When Joseph took up his, a dove flew out of it and landed on his head. But he remarks he is an old man and already has children.

Chapter sixteen says that the priest gave the water of the ordeal to Joseph and Mary, but they remained unhurt. So no judgment was passed on them.

Chapters seventeen and eighteen state that Joseph took Mary and his sons with him to Bethlehem to be registered. Joseph found a cave for Mary to give birth in *before* they came into Bethlehem.

Demonic Gospels

Chapter nineteen says that the infant Jesus just *appeared* after a bright light shone in the cave.

Chapter twenty states that the midwife, Salome, went to check to see if Mary was really still virgin, and her hand became severely burned. Then an angel appeared and she believed. After that, the angel healed her hand.

Chapter twenty-one says that the Magi were in Bethlehem before Joseph and Mary got there. They visited Jesus in the cave (contradicting the Magi's own account. See Matthew 2:11).

> "Those who wish to preserve the honor of Mary in virginity to the end, say, basing it on a tradition in the Gospel according to Peter, as it is entitled, or "The Book of James," (Protevangelium Jacobi, c. 9) that the brethren of Jesus were sons of Joseph by a former wife, whom he married before Mary."
> Origen, *Commentary on Matthew 10.17*

Other Gnostic Gospels

Gospel of the Hebrews
This work no longer exists. All we know about it comes from the writings of the ancient church fathers. It was known as a Gnostic work and in one section it said Jesus confessed the (female) Holy Spirit as His true mother.

> "Many dispute the *Gospel of the Hebrews*."
> Origen, *Commentary on John 2.6*

> "The "prayer of Joseph" is indeed included in the *Gospel of the Hebrews*, but many doubt its authenticity." Origen, *Commentary on John 2.25*

> "The *Gospel of the Hebrews*...and the *Gospel of the Egyptians* are disputed by most.
> Clement of Alexandria, *Stromata 3.10*

Secret Gospel of Mark
There was a fragment of a letter reportedly from Clement of Alexandria to Theodore that mentions a secret gospel of Mark. This Gnostic forgery was a creation of the Carpocratian Gnostics. It said that Christians should be ready to deny that it is a real gospel and explain why. The actual *Secret Gospel of Mark* no longer exists.

Gospel of the Nativity of Mary
This Gnostic work is nearly identical with that of *Pseudo-Matthew*. It may have been written by the same Gnostic.

Demonic Gospels

Below is what church father Jerome stated about this work.

> "You ask me to let you know what I think of a book held by some to be about the nativity of St. Mary; and so I wish you to know that there is much in it that is false. For one Seleucus composed this book. But, just as he wrote what was true about their powers, and the miracles they worked, but said a great deal that was false about their doctrine."
> *Jerome's Second Letter to Bishop Cromatius*

Gospel of Peter
This Gnostic work was used by Docetists. Docetism is the Gnostic belief that Jesus was a phantasm, meaning He did not have a physical body. At first it appears to be the same account as the gospel of Mark. But when we look at it more closely we see that Jesus did not resurrect in a physical body, and did not leave footprints in the sand. Church father Theodoret states that it was very close to the *Gospel of the Hebrews*, and that both were heretical.

History of Joseph the Carpenter
This work tells of the permanent virginity of Mary and her marriage to Joseph at the age of twelve. It reported that Joseph had four boys and two girls by a previous marriage. It mentioned that Joseph was a priest in the temple (even though that would be forbidden since he was from the tribe of Judah, not Levi). It applies the prophecies of not one bone being broken and of his body

Other Gnostic Gospels

not seeing corruption, to Joseph instead of Jesus. It taught there will be four witnesses killed by the Antichrist, not two, specifically Enoch, Elijah, Schila, and Tabia.

There are other false gospels listed in volume eight of the *Ante Nicene Fathers* under Apocryphal Gospels and Acts.

Gnostic Epistles

Apocalypse of Peter

There are two Greek versions and one Ethiopic version of the *Apocalypse of Peter*. Each is quite different in several points, but they all have a common storyline. This work is also called the *Revelation of Peter*.

This work begins with Jesus and the disciples on the Mount of Olives. Jesus begins a discourse about the end of the world with Peter asking Him questions. In response, Jesus gives Peter three visions.

The first vision is that of Pharisees attacking Peter. Jesus explains the vision by saying that there are three types of people: those who are immortal, those who start to believe but fall way, and those who will never understand. Peter must be careful who he tells some of his visions to. This teaching corresponds to the Valentinian Gnostic idea of the three types of people: the physics, pneumatics, and the hyle.

In Peter's second vision Jesus shows him how he can conquer the unbelieving Pharisees by gnosis but not without many dangers.

Peter has a third vision of the torments of hell and the pleasures of heaven. This work is gently saying there will be a war between the Christians (symbolized by Peter and his authority) and the Gnostics.

Demonic Gospels

Clement of Alexandria stated some Christians used the *Apocalypse of Peter* but most Christians considered all the supposed versions of the apocalypse to be fake. We are not sure which one of the texts Clement was referring to, just that it was one of the three that still exist, or, possibly, some of other unknown version.

> "We receive the Apocalypses of John and Peter only. Some of us do not wish the Apocalypse of Peter to be read in church."
> *Muratorian Canon Fragment*

Apocryphon of James

The word "apocryphon" is normally used to mean an apocryphal or fake apocalypse. In other words, it is usually used to denote a book of false predictions. This Gnostic work is also called the *Secret Book of James*. The ancient church fathers consistently taught there never were any secret teachings of Jesus, but everything was proclaimed and written out for all to see and be saved.

The manuscript begins with Jesus pulling Peter and James aside and sharing some secret teachings that only they would understand.

He teaches that they must become full of the Spirit; then they can become completely equal to Jesus, becoming sons of the Holy Spirit. He also supposedly said that prophecy stopped with John the Baptist, so they should not concern themselves with it. Instead of worrying about what is to come, Jesus said they should concern themselves with how to defeat the archons. True revelation is the enlightenment of your divinity through gnosis.

This work ends by Jesus saying another one is coming who is greater than He, and to earnestly seek to make themselves one with his followers and proclaim a portion with them. Then they will be truly sons of the Lord.

Demonic Gospels

Daniel 11 shows how the Antichrist will claim to be a Christ and worship a god of forces. Jesus referred to the Antichrist when He said:

> "I am come in my Father's name, and ye receive me not: if another shall come in his own name, him ye will receive." *John 5:43*

So this Gnostic work is actually leading people toward accepting the Antichrist.

Apocryphon of John

This Gnostic work is also called the *Secret Book of John*. There are three different versions of this work. It is a story of the risen Christ explaining to His disciple John how all things came to be. He tells the Gnostic version of the Creation and about the creation and fall of the goddess Sophia.

The Gnostic gospel message in this work is that Adam was created with the divine spark in him. When Eve was created and Adam desired her sexually, some of the light became trapped causing the fall of man. Jesus incarnated into this world to teach the good news of each man's divinity. Those who realize this through the ascetic lifestyle of Gnostic meditation will return to the pleroma (the Gnostic heaven, the realm of perfection). Those who do not, will continue to be trapped in an endless cycle of reincarnation.

It also teaches that the true creator and giver of eternal life is the Monad, the eternal Father, Mother, and Son.

In this gospel we see the Gnostic teaching that multiple gods, a female Holy Spirit, reincarnation, and sorcery are the answers to eternal life.

Book of Thomas the Contender

This text presents a conversation between the risen Jesus and the disciple Thomas. In this text, Jesus refers to Thomas as his "brother," "twin," and "friend."

We have seen that some Gnostic groups taught that Jesus and Mary Magdalene were the emanations of the Logos and Sophia. Saying Jesus had a fraternal twin may have been another way of describing the incarnation of twin powers; but as we know, that idea contradicts the four canonical gospels.

Another possible reason for calling Thomas the twin of Jesus, would be to say Thomas became a twin to Jesus spiritually in that he obtained the christ-conscience and was now a christ. This would fit perfectly with Gnostic teaching, but it is still heresy.

The text does state that Thomas was about to discover what he himself really was. It also seems to indicate that sex will lead one astray from their knowledge of their own godhood.

In John 20 we see Thomas believing in Jesus' real physical resurrection, not reincarnation, as the Gnostics believed.

Dialogue of the Savior

This Gnostic work begins with Jesus addressing His three most Gnosticly perfect disciples: Mary Magdalene, Matthew, and Judas. Later in the work all the other disciples are present. There are many missing parts from the parchment, so there are several gaps in the story. It contains Gnostic versions of the Creation, baptismal regeneration, and the ascent of the soul upward through the powers of darkness. The soul's ascent is accomplished by obtaining a singleness of mind through meditative gnosis.

This work also mentions the *Gospel of the Egyptians* contains secret wisdom given by the Savior. It further teaches that the Naassenes (a Gnostic sect) are worthy of study.

Some odd teachings of Jesus are:
1. There are no earthquakes; the earth never moves.
2. Do not seek the garment of the archons and angels.
3. It is good to remove your earthy garment when you choose to do so (suicide is permissible and sometimes preferable).
4. When you pray, pray where there are no females present.
5. One day all females will dissolve (which is why they must become male).

Demonic Gospels

6. Jesus sated: "I have come to destroy the works of the female." (This probably refers to ceasing the cycle of reincarnation.)
7. Judas has eternal life abiding in him.

Epistle of the Apostles

The *Epistle of the Apostles* reports to be another story of the Apostles and the teachings of Jesus. It may have some real truth to it; but it has obviously been tampered with. The Coptic version begins with chapter 7.

Teachings that match the Bible are:
    Jesus is God (chapter 3) and that "all men have the power to believe" (chapter 39).

One can see the Gnostic influence in:
    Chapter 4, which contains the infancy gospel story of the letters A and B (See *Gospel of Thomas*).
    Chapter 11 shows Jesus telling Andrew, Peter, and Thomas to look at His hands and feet and side. Jesus then says: "for it is written in the prophet: A phantom of a devil makes no footprint on the earth."
    Chapter 13 tells of Jesus' descent to earth, changing forms so the angels and others don't realize He is descending.
    Chapter 14 says Jesus appeared as Gabriel to Mary.
    Chapter 15 supposedly records Jesus saying it is needful to keep the Passover until He comes again.
    Chapter 17 uses the word Ogdoad and has Gnostic flavor to it.
    Chapter 28 uses the word archons for evil rulers.

Chapter 42 - The five wise virgins are "Faith and Love and Grace and Peace and Hope" and the foolish are "Knowledge, Understanding (Perception), Obedience, Patience, and Compassion." Those foolish ones are those "that have believed and confessed Me but have not fulfilled My commandments."

There is a false prophecy in chapter 17 stating that the Second Coming will be 150 or 120 years after Pentecost. This, of course, did not happen.

Letter of Peter to Philip

This Gnostic work starts out with Peter at odds with Philip. Peter writes a letter to Philip to come and fellowship with the other apostles and seek the Lord's will. Philip agrees and all the disciples gather together and go to the Mount of Olives to pray. Peter prays to the Lord to reveal to them how to defeat the "the deficiency of the aeons and their pleroma."

A light comes down from heaven and Jesus, who no longer has a physical body, appears. Jesus tells them the deficiency was caused from the fall of the mother (the goddess Sophia) when she created the aeons without permission. They in turn created the pleroma and the arrogant one (the God of the Old Testament).

Peter asks, "How do we fight against the aeons?" Jesus explains that "When you strip off from yourselves what is corrupted, then you will become illuminators in the midst of mortal men." Jesus went on to say the process is by teaching the world this "salvation with a promise." The promise is defined as the authority to "enter into the inheritance of fatherhood." In other words, they defeat the aeons by teaching people to meditate back into the light of the father and enter into their own godhood.

Pistis Sophia

This Gnostic work was a highly valued manuscript by the Valentinian Gnostics. It teaches reincarnation in general and, specifically, that John the Baptist was a reincarnation of Elijah the prophet. It teaches that the angelic being known a Melchizedek is actually the light purifier, or Lucifer, who aids in our true salvation.

Jesus tells the story of how the aeons (supreme gods) created the goddess Sophia. Sophia, without permission, emanated (created a being by putting part of herself into it) the God of the Old Testament. He created the earth and Adam and Eve but enslaved them. To rectify this issue, the aeons created Jesus, who was equal to Sophia. Sophia and Jesus would incarnate into human form and show the way of salvation to humans. This story is called the fall, repentance, and restoration of Sophia.

Then there are forty-six questions asked mostly by Mary.

The text leads one to believe that the Christ-consciousness descended on Jesus and the Sophia-consciousness descended on Mary Magdalene. Together the couple would be complete, able to teach others how to save themselves through gnosis.

Ptolemy's Letter to Flora

This work was preserved by a fourth-century church father named Epiphanius of Salamis.

The small work is a personal letter from a Valentinian Gnostic to a Christian woman named Flora. In this letter Ptolemy agrees that it is necessary to read and understand the Hebrew Scriptures. What she must understand is that the God of the Old Testament, who created the material world and gave the Law to Moses, is just. However, He is just, not perfect. Christians believe the Creator to be the only God who exists and is perfect and good. Most Gnostics believe He is an evil and demented god. They refuse to serve Him; but instead serve a higher god.

Ptolemy came to the conclusion that neither is true. He does believe there are more perfect gods and goddesses, like Sophia. But he believes the Creator of the material world is a good and just God, just not perfect.

Ptolemy gives several examples which he believes prove that the Old Testament God is not perfect and reliable. He relied more on his visions or experiences.

Revelation of Paul

There are two apocryphal books bearing the name of the apostle Paul. The *Revelation of Paul*, also called the *Apocalypse of Paul* and the *Vision of Paul*, is recorded by church fathers Augustine and Sozomen as forged works. Numerous others cite the *Revelation of Paul*. One stated it was a forgery by the heretic Paul of Samosata, the founder of the sect of the Gnostic Paulicians. Its own introduction describes how it was supposed to have been found under the foundation of the original house of Paul the apostle. It contradicts the Scripture in several places.

In the first paragraph:
We learn we are supposed to command God to burn up sinners. The moon and stars talk to God. Holy men spend their lives fasting, and sin is only found in matter (a common Gnostic teaching).

In the second paragraph:
One must remember where their body was left when they die, so they can get back into it at the resurrection. Everyone will go to a place of rest or to a place of fire depending on their works.

In the third paragraph:
At death Christians will be thrown into the Acherusian Lake by Michael the archangel, as a baptism. Only then can they go into the city of God.

In the fifth paragraph:
People are judged according to their works. (This contradicts Paul in Romans 4)

In the sixth paragraph:
People will be tortured in hell if they do not confess that Holy Mary is the mother of God, that the Lord did not take His humanity from her, and that the Eucharist actually changes into the physical flesh and blood of God.

Sophia of Jesus Christ

This work retells the Gnostic idea of the unknowable father who created the archons, Sophia, and the Christ. Sophia made a mistake and fell, thereby creating the demiurge who created the material world, all the evil creator angels, and man. Sophia sought to rectify her mistake by sending the serpent into the garden in order to give man and woman a spark of the divine so they could obtain christhood. To complete the work of redemption, the Christ and Sophia incarnated in the forms of Jesus and Mary Magdalene. Salvation is by the process of gnosis (Gnostic mediation), not by Jesus' death on the cross.

This is the same message given in the *Gospel of the Egyptians* and the *Apocryphon of John*.

Other Gnostic Epistles

Acts of the Apostles
This is a fake work with the same title as the biblical book of Acts. It no longer exists.

> "It [Pseudo-Matthew] was published by a disciple of Manichæus named Leucius, who also wrote the falsely styled *Acts of the Apostles*."
> Jerome's First Letter to Bishop Cromatius

Acts of Paul
The *Acts of Paul* and the *Acts of Paul and Thecla* are often found together. Origen mentions the *Acts of Paul* denying the divinity of Christ. Some of the doctrinal problems with these works are: baptism is necessary for salvation, God will bless married people if they remain celibate, God speaks only to virgins, and at death, saints will become angels.

> "The language which is found in the *Acts of Paul*, where it is said that "here is the Word a living being," [denying Jesus' divinity]... take care that you be not guilty of impiety against the unbegotten Father Himself."
> Origen, *Of First Principles 1:2:3*

Acts of Paul and Thecla
In addition to the above-mentioned doctrines, this part of the work suggests that women can baptize, teach, and hold authority over men.

> "But if the writings which wrongly go under Paul's name [*Acts of Paul and Thecla*], claim Thecla's example as a license for women's teaching and baptizing, let them know that, in Asia, the presbyter who composed that writing, as if he were augmenting Paul's fame from his own store, after being convicted, and confessing that he had done it from love of Paul, was removed from his office." Tertullian, *On Baptism 17*

Apocalypse of Adam
This work reports to be Adam's revelations to his son Seth. The text talks about the archons, worlds of angels and other godlike beings, and salvation though gnosis. No actual prophecy is given.

Apocalypse of the Virgin
This work reports to be the visions of the Virgin Mary, the mother of God. She sees and describes which torment is given to each kind of sinner in hell. This work is similar to the *Revelation of Paul*.

Ascension of Paul
The *Ascension of Paul* was written by the Cainite Gnostics and reports how Paul ascended to godhood through Gnostic meditation.

Other Gnostic Epistles

Book of Alcibades

This work was used by the Gnostic Elchasaites. It teaches that there are female angels. It also says that a true remission of sins can only be accomplished by the ritual contained in this book.[a] To my knowledge this book no longer exits, but it is logical to assume that "the remission of sins" in this work has to do with Gnostic meditation.

Book of Revelations

This work has the same name as the Bible book of Revelation, except it is plural. It is a work written by a false prophetess named Philumese. Her work was used by the Gnostic Apelles, who taught Jesus came in the flesh (unlike most Gnostics), but after the resurrection, Jesus disintegrated His own body.[b] This unique Gnostic doctrine is still taught by the modern Jehovah's Witness cult.

> "Apelles devoted his attention to a book entitled *Revelations*, written by a certain woman named Philumene, whom he considers to be a prophetess."
> Hippolytus, *Refutation of all Heresies 10.16*

The book is mainly a text of random Scriptures separated by the phrase "be still and know that I am God." It is designed to be used for Gnostic meditation.

---

[a] Hippolytus, *Heresies 9.8-9*
[b] Hippolytus, *Heresies 7.26*

Demonic Gospels

Epistle of Laodiceans and the Epistle of Alexandrians
We must remember that there is a *real* epistle of Paul to the Laodiceans mentioned in Colossians 4:16. These two works, however, were fake epistles written by presbyters to counter the Gnostic heresies.

> "There are also circulating one [epistle] to the Laodiceans and one to the Alexandrians, forged in the name of Paul against the heresy of Marcion. *Muratorian Canon Fragment*

Exegesis on the Soul
This is a description of how the soul is freed from the bondage of death and beginning the process of obtaining godhood by the sacrament of the bridal chamber.

> "The soul awaits for the true bridegroom to ascend in the bridal chamber that she has filled with perfume and cleansed herself."

First Book of Adam and Eve
There are different versions of this work. The Gnostic version details what supposedly happened to Adam and Eve upon their expulsion from the Garden of Eden. They did not eat food for several months because they could not find any. Adam suggested they pay penance by standing in a river for days. Satan tricked Eve out of finishing the penance, so they could not completely pay for their sins. The angels originally worshiped Adam as the only image of God. Adam was buried in Paradise. Seth then assumes

Other Gnostic Epistles

the leadership of man and wrote the words of God on tablets of stone.

Hypostasis of the Archons
This Gnostic work consists of a person asking questions about subjects found in Genesis. An angel answers these questions in an esoteric style. It contains references to Sophia's fall.

Melchizedek
This Gnostic treatise teaches that Melchizedek is Jesus Christ. He came, preached gnosis, died, and resurrected (spiritually, not going through any more cycles of reincarnation). His second coming will be with the help of the other gods, when He is made priest / king.

New Book of Psalms
This work no longer exists, but it is mentioned in the *Muratorian Canon Fragment*.

> "We reject everything written by Arsenus, Valentinus, or Miltiadees. We also reject those who wrote the *New Book of Psalms*, Marcion, Basilides, the founder of the Asian Cataphrigians and..." *Muratorian Canon Fragment*

On the Origin of the World
This Gnostic work was written about the fourth century. It deals with the cosmology of the universe and the Gnostic idea about Sophia's fall. It also talks about the end times, but no actual prophecy is given.

Demonic Gospels

Paraphrase of Seth
This work no longer exists, to my knowledge, but the ancient church fathers classified it as Gnostic heresy.

> "The *Paraphrase of Seth* is the official doctrine of the Gnostic Sethites."
> Hippolytus, *Refutation of all Heresies 5.17*

Second Book of Adam and Eve
The second book continues where the other left off. It describes how the descendants of Cain grew evil and became known as Fallen (Nephilim), while the sons of Seth were known as the "Sons of God" and "angels," and remained virtuous and dwelt on a mountain top isolated from the descendants of Cain. Eventually all the descendants of Seth, except for Noah and his family who remained on the mountain, descended from the mountain and joined the Fallen. It teaches that female angels and Aeons exist.

This book gave rise to the idea that the Sethites were the "sons of God" in Genesis 6 and that the Cainites were the "daughters of men." Parts of the books of Adam and Eve can be found in Muslim legends and in the Quran itself.

Second and Third Enoch
Many of the ancient church fathers spoke highly of the *Book of Enoch*. It is even quoted in Jude 14-15. Unlike the biblically referenced *Book of Enoch*, however, these are Gnostic forgeries in Enoch's name.

> "*Second Enoch* and the *Secrets of Enoch* are not considered sacred by the church."
> Origen, *Against Celsus 5:48*

> "The *Book of Enoch* is genuine Scripture. It is not received by some, because it is not admitted into the Jewish canon, either. The Jews rejected it like other portions of Scripture, because it testifies of Christ. The fact that Jude quotes it is proof enough." Tertullian, *Apparel of Women 1.3*

Sentences of Sextus

This work is a collection of sayings like the Gnostic gospels of Thomas and Philip. It contains what is called its "sentences" for the use of Gnostic meditation. The wisdom sayings are from Sextus rather than Jesus. Sextus may have been a Pythagorean Gnostic.

Shepherd of Hermas

This work does not seem to be directly Gnostic in origin, but it was often used by the Gnostics.

> "The *Shepherd of Hermas* is a treatise, not inspired Scripture."
> Origen, *Of First Principles 1:3:3*

> "But Hermas wrote *the Shepherd* in the city of Rome most recently in our times, when his brother, bishop Pious, was occupying the chair in the church at Rome. And so indeed it ought to be read; but that it be made public to the people in

Demonic Gospels

the church and placed among the prophets whose number is complete, or among the apostles, is not possible to the end of time."
Muratorian Canon Fragment

Summer Harvest
A mystical poem written by the Gnostic Valentinus, founder of the Valentinian Gnostic Movement.

Teaching of Peter, Preaching of Peter
The *Teaching of Peter*, or the *Preaching of Peter* as it is also called, is a work that teaches that the god the Greeks worship is the same as the God worshiped by the Jews. We should not use idols like the Greeks, but not worship in the manner of the Jews, either.

"The *Preaching of Peter*... was not included among the ecclesiastical books. For we can show that it was not composed by Peter or by any other person inspired by the Holy Spirit."
Origen *Of First Principles 1.8*

"If anyone should quote to us out of the little treatise entitled the *Teaching of Peter* (also called the *Preaching of Peter*)... I have to reply, in the first place, that this work is not included among the ecclesiastical books. For we can show it was not composed either by Peter nor any other person inspired by the Spirit of God."
Origen, *Of First Principles; preface 8*

Other Gnostic Epistles

Third and Fourth Beruch
Third Beruch is supposed to be a vision seen by Beruch, the scribe of Jeremiah the prophet. It tells the story of a great dragon that eats the people who are sent to hell, and of a fire bird who absorbs the fire of the sun so the earth is not burned. *Fourth Beruch* tells the story of how God did not want Beruch to see the destruction of Jerusalem, so He caused him to fall asleep for sixty-six years. It does mention the "light of the aeons."

> "The Gnostic Justinus gets his teachings from *Third* and *Fourth Beruch*."
> Hippolytus, *Refutation of all Heresies 5.19*

Tripartite Tractate
This Gnostic work teaches that there are three types of human beings. There are psychics who have a divine spark within them. They are born predestined for christhood or godhood. There are the pneumatics who, if they practice enough good work and rituals, may be able to ascend back into the pleroma (Gnostic heaven). Finally, there are the hyle. Hylic people are completely bound to matter and incapable of being saved. They are destined for destruction.

Treatise on the Resurrection
This small work gives the Gnostic definition of what the resurrection really is. It is not the physical resurrection of the body that Christians teach, but a spiritual one where one puts on the godhood.

Demonic Gospels

Conclusion

There are other false epistles listed in Volume 8 of the Ante-Nicene Fathers under apocryphal gospels and acts. These are not necessarily Gnostic, but are considered fake works because they present a different gospel with a different plan of salvation than the Bible does.

Avenging of the Savior
Acts of Peter and Paul
Acts of Paul and Thecla
Acts of Barnabas
Acts of Philip
Martyrdom of Andrew
Acts of Andrew and Matthias
Acts of Peter and Andrew
Acts and Martyrdom of Matthew
Acts of Thomas
Consummation of Thomas
Martyrdom of Bartholomew
Acts of Thaddeus
Acts of John
Revelation of Moses
Revelation of Esdras
Revelation of John
Prayer of the Apostle Paul
Teachings of Silvanus

Dead Sea Scrolls

The Dead Sea Scrolls produced and protected by the Essene community at Qumran, show us a godly library. In contrast, the Gnostic scrolls produced by the Gnostic Egyptians in Nag Hammadi are the epitome of a satanic library.

Qumran - The Dead Sea Scrolls
Qumran has Scripture, commentaries, and cultic books (astrological) just as any good minister would have for the purpose of getting his facts straight and witnessing.

In the commentaries, the phrase "it is written" often appears. Anyone who carefully studies this will see that phrase is only applied to what they know to be the true Scripture. It is never applied to any other type of writing, even their own community rule! This lets us know they believed in the inspiration of Scripture and tells us which books they considered to be Scripture.

Some say that the Dead Sea Scrolls included the Apocrypha or that only about 40 to 60 percent of the Dead Sea Scrolls agree with the Received Text. This is true only if we lump all the scrolls together. However, if we remove the commentaries, paraphrases, Greek texts, cult witnessing scrolls, and the like, we will see the same Old Testament we have today. About 98% of those Dead Sea Scrolls agree with the Received Text.

Demonic Gospels

The Books of the Dead Sea Scrolls

True Scripture
The whole Old Testament except Esther (to date)

Commentaries
Habakkuk, Hosea, Isaiah, Micah, Nahum, Psalms, Song of Solomon, and Zephaniah

Paraphrases
Genesis, Exodus LXX, Exodus, Joshua, Leviticus, and Job

Prophecy
Damascus Document, The Instruction, Messianic Anthology, Messianic Apocalypse, Melchizedek fragment, Midrash on the Last Days, The Mysteries, MMT (Miqsat Ma'ase ha-Torah), The New Jerusalem, Priestly Prophecy, Son of God Apocalypse

Community Related
Calendrical Document, Community Rule Scroll, Copper Scroll, Festival Prayers, Temple Scroll, Thanksgiving Hymns, Three Tongues of Fire, Rule of Blessing, Rule of the Congregation, Songs of King Jonathan, Songs of Sabbath Sacrifice, Songs of the Sage, War Scroll

Miscellaneous Works
Allegory of the Vine, Apocryphon of Moses, Apocryphon of David, Apocryphon of Malachi, Apocryphon on Samuel-Kings, Book of Giants, Book of Noah, Enoch,

Genesis Apocryphon, Words of Michael the Archangel, Book of War, Jubilees, Sirach, Tobit, Baruch, and the Testaments of Levi, Judah, Naphtali, and Joseph.

Useful Extra-Biblical Books

There are a few true ancient books that are a help in understanding the past. The first ones we should look at are those that are recommended by Scripture itself.

Lost Works
These are works mentioned by the Bible or the ancient church fathers that currently do not exist. If anyone discovers any of these works, please let us know so that they can be published in easy-to-read English.

1. Book of the Wars of the Lord (Numbers 21:14)
2. Book of Jasher (Joshua 10:13)
3. Annals of Jehu (2 Chronicles 20:34)
4. Treatise of the Book of the Kings (2 Chronicles 24:27)
5. Chronicles of Kings (Esther 2:23; 6:1)
6. Acts of Solomon (1 Kings 11:41)
7. Sayings of the Seers (2 Chronicles 33:19)
8. Chronicles of King David (1 Chronicles 27:24)
9. Chronicles of Gad the Seer (1 Chronicles 29:29)
10. Treatise of the Prophet Iddo (2 Chronicles 13:22)
11. Prophecy of Ahijah the Shilonite (2 Chronicles 9:29)
12. Records of Nathan the Prophet (2 Chronicles 9:29)
13. Book of Samuel the Seer (1 Chronicles 29:29)

Book of Jasher
The only one of the thirteen books recommended by Scripture that still exists is the *Book of Jasher*, quoted by

Useful Extra-Biblical Books

name in Joshua 10:13 and 2 Samuel 1:18. Paul mentioned the names of the magicians who withstood Moses in 2 Timothy 3:8. Their names are only found in the book of Jasher, so we know he was quoting from it. Jasher gives extra information about the time period between Creation and the death of Joshua, the first 2,516 years of human history.

Epistle of Barnabas

This *Epistle of Barnabas* was preserved by the ancient church. It was very highly thought of by most of the ancient church fathers and quoted often. It mainly teaches about the typological prophecies of Scripture. It clearly teaches the Jews would return to the land of Israel and rebuild their temple in the last days.

Josephus

Josephus was a Jewish historian who wrote about the time of the fall of Jerusalem in AD 70. He recorded some useful new information from the time period of Creation to the destruction of the Temple. The second half of his work deals mostly with the Roman Empire.

Seder Olam

This Jewish history book was compiled about AD 167. It is one of the main sources the Talmud uses for its chronology.

Third Corinthians

The ancient church fathers believed Paul to have written four epistles to Corinth. Two were canonized as First and

Demonic Gospels

Second Corinthians. One is lost to us. And this one was preserved by the Arminian Church. It does not give much new information, but reveals the Gnostic problem well. It also contains a prophecy that Gnostic heresy will return and be a major problem in the last days.

Book of Enoch
The *Book of Enoch* is mentioned in Jude. It was preserved by the Ethiopian church and found among the Dead Sea Scrolls. It reports to be a book kept especially for the end times.

Book of Jubilees
This is a document found among the Dead Sea Scrolls that tries to fill in the gaps of the Genesis record. It does not contradict Scripture, but *does* contradict some the information found in the book of Jasher.

Ante-Nicene Church Fathers
Finally, we come to the collection of the writings of the ancient church. These are all the writings that still existed in the late nineteenth century, compiled into ten volumes. These require a lot of time to study, but it is well worth the effort.

Eusebius
Eusebius was called the Father of Church History. He gave a great synopsis of the ante-Nicene fathers in only one volume.

Conclusion

The Scriptures prove themselves by fulfilled prophecy. Any other document, Gnostic or not, that contradicts the Scriptures historically, doctrinally, or in any other way, is demonic. These demonic documents should be ignored.

Appendix A
Modern Prophecy

Twenty of the fifty-five prophecies fulfilled in modern times occurred in the year 1948 itself. It was prophesied that the British (Tarshish) would begin to bring the Jews back to establish their nation. It was also prophesied that the Jews would return to the land of Israel under the leadership of someone named after King David (David Ben Gurion). The exact date of Israel's establishment was foretold. Immediately after Israel's establishment, Moab (modern Jordan) was supposed to attack and take Israeli territory (creating what we call the West Bank). The Eastern Gate of the Temple Mount would remain sealed. The Israeli flag would display the Star of David. The ancient language of Hebrew was revived as prophesied. The ancient cities have been revived and renamed their original Hebrew names. Five cites were prophesied to remain desolate for all time and are still desolate. Also, the renewed land would be named Israel, not Judah. Both nations would be one again.

Eight wars between Israel and Syria were predicted, four of which have already been fulfilled. The cities of Ashdod and Ashkelon were rebuilt as prophesied. The shekel was recreated for Israeli currency. The forests have reappeared in Israel. In AD 2004 the Sanhedrin was reestablished as prophesied.

Appendix A - Modern Prophecy

Many other prophecies have been fulfilled involving wars, certain cities, and people who were named and/or described in such detail it is absolutely impossible for it all to be a coincidence!

1948

Israel will be reestablished as a nation (Isa. 11:11)
British ships will be the first to bring the Jewish people home (Isa. 60:9)
Israel will come back as one nation, not two (Hosea 1:11; Ezk. 37:18, 19, 22)
The nation of Israel will be born in a day (Isa. 66:8)
Israel will be reestablished by a leader named David (Hosea 3:5)
The revived state will be named "Israel" (Ezek. 37:11)
The Star of David will be on the Israeli flag (Isa. 11:10)
The nation will be reestablished in the ancient land of Canaan (Jer. 30:2, 3; Ezk. 37:12)
Israel will no longer speak of being freed from Egypt (Jer. 16:14, 15)
Israel will not be restored as a monarchy (Mic. 5:5)
Israel will be established on the date predicted (Dan 4; Ezk. 4:4-6)
The Hebrew language will be revived in Israel (Jer. 31:23)
Jerusalem will be divided (Zech. 14:1-3)
Jordan will occupy the West Bank (Zeph. 2:8; Zech. 12:1-7)
Israel will be initially restored without Jerusalem (Zech. 12:1-7)

Israel will have a fierce military (firepot) (Zech. 12:1-7; Isa. 41)
Dead Sea Scrolls will be found (Isa. 29:1-4)
Israel will be reestablished by the fourth craftsman (Zech. 1:18-21)
The Jewish people will return in unbelief (Ezk. 37:7-8, 11)
First Shepherd will arise (Mic. 5:5-8)

1949
Yemenite Jews will return (Isa. 43:3-7)

1951
Israel will control Ashkelon (Zech. 9:1-8)

1953
Egypt will no longer have kings (Zech. 10:9-11)

1967
Second Shepherd will arise (Mic. 5:5-8)
The 1967 war will occur on the date predicted (Dan. 5)
Five Egyptian cities will be conquered by the Israelis (Isa. 19:16-18)
Jordan will give up the West Bank (Zech. 12:6)
West Bank Jews will go home to Jerusalem (Zech. 12:6)

1968
Israel will control Ashdod (Zech. 9:1-8)

1973
Yom Kippur War will occur (Mic. 5:5-8)

Appendix A - Modern Prophecy

Jerusalem will be a burden to all nations (Zech. 12:2, 3)

1980
The shekel will be revived as Israeli currency (Ezk. 45:1-2)

1981
Third Shepherd will arise (Mic. 5:5-8)

1982
Israel will give back the Sinai Peninsula (Zech. 10:6)
First Lebanese War will occur (firepot) (Zech. 12:6)

1989
The Berlin Wall will fall (Ezk. 38:4-6)

1990
Ethiopian Jews will be brought to Israel (Isa. 18:1-7)

~2000
Cities will be restored and Israel will have non-Jewish farmers (Isa. 61:4, 5; Zeph. 2)
Jerusalem will grow beyond its old walls (Zech. 2:4, 5)
Land of Israel will be divided by its rivers and by Muslims (Isa. 18:1-7)
Tourists will fly in and support Israel (Isa. 60:8-10; Isa. 61)
There will be constant planting and reaping (crops) (Amos 9:13-15)
Forests will reappear in Israel (cedar, etc.) (Isa. 41:18-20)
Desolate land and cities will be restored (Ezk. 36:33-36)
Five cities will stay desolate (Matt. 11:20-24)

Demonic Gospels

Muslims will not "reckon Israel among nations" (Num. 23:9)
Israel will inherit remnant of Edom /Palestinians (Amos 9:12)
Satellite-Television Communication Systems Invented (Rev. 17:8)

2004
Sanhedrin will be reestablished (Matt. 24:15, 20)

2005
Palestinians will want Jerusalem as their capital (Ezk. 36:2, 7, 10-11)
Gaza will be forsaken (Zeph. 2:4)
Russia and Iran will sign a military defense pact (Ezk. 38:3-8)

2006
Second Lebanese War will occur (Psalm 83:1-18)

2011
Russia and Turkey will sign a military defense pact (Ezk. 38:3-8)

You should notice that all these fifty-five fulfilled prophecies are from the Old Testament. None are found in the New Testament. This has led some to conclude that modern Judaism holds the complete truth and people should reject Christianity. But this same Old Testament clearly proves that Jesus is the Messiah who was

Appendix A - Modern Prophecy

supposed to come before the destruction of the second temple by Titus in AD 70.

Fifteen prophecies yet to occur are given below.
The West Bank will become an independent state (Dan. 11:45)
Fourth Shepherd's Syrian war will occur (Mic. 5:1-8)
Fifth Shepherd's Syrian war will occur (Mic. 5:1-8)
Lebanon-Jordan war will occur (Zech. 10-11; Obad. 1:19)
Sephardic Jews will return to Israel & populate the Negev (Obad. 1:20)
Sixth Shepherd's Syrian war will occur (Mic. 5:1-8)
Damascus will be destroyed (Isa. 17:1)
Gog-Magog War will occur immediately after Israel wins another war (Ezek. 38)
Rise of the ten nations to occur after the Gog-Magog War (Dan. 8, 11)
Increased understanding of prophecies will occur (Dan. 12:40
Children will be rebellious and society will be materialistic (Mark 13:12; 1 Tim. 3:23)
Jesus' words will never be forgotten (Mat. 24:15)
Christians will be hated for Jesus' name's sake (Luke 21:17)
The apostasy of the church will fully form (2 Thess. 2:9-12)
The Rapture of the believing church will occur (1Thes. 4:17)
The seven-year Tribulation will begin (Dan. 9:27)

Chart adapted from *Ancient Prophecies Revealed*.

Other Books by Ken Johnson, Th.D.

Ancient Post-Flood History
Historical Documents That Point to a Biblical Creation.
This book is a Christian timeline of ancient post-Flood history based on Bible chronology, the early church fathers, and ancient Jewish and secular history. This can be used as a companion guide in the study of Creation Science. Some questions answered: Who were the Pharaohs in the times of Joseph and Moses? When did the famine of Joseph occur? What Egyptian documents mention these? When did the Exodus take place? When did the Kings of Egypt start being called "Pharaoh" and why? Who was the first king of a united Italy? Who was Zeus and where is he buried? Where did Shem and Ham rule and where are they buried? How large was Nimrod's invasion force that set up the Babylonian Empire, and when did this invasion occur? What is Nimrod's name in Persian documents? How can we use this information to witness to unbelievers?

Ancient Seder Olam
A Christian Translation of the 2000-year-old Scroll
This 2000-year-old scroll reveals the chronology from Creation through Cyrus' decree that freed the Jews in 536 BC. The Ancient Seder Olam uses biblical prophecy to prove its calculations of the timeline. We have used this technique to continue the timeline all the way to the reestablishment of the nation of Israel in AD 1948. Using the Bible and rabbinical tradition, this book shows that the ancient Jews awaited King Messiah to fulfill the prophecy spoken of in Daniel, Chapter 9. The Seder answers many questions about the chronology of the books of Kings and Chronicles. It talks about the coming of Elijah, King Messiah's reign, and the battle of Gog and Magog.

Ancient Prophecies Revealed
500 Prophecies Listed In Order Of When They Were Fulfilled

This book details over 500 biblical prophecies in the order they were fulfilled; these include pre-flood times though the First Coming of Jesus and into the Middle Ages. The heart of this book is the 53 prophecies fulfilled between 1948 and 2008. The last 11 prophecies between 2008 and the Tribulation are also given. All these are documented and interpreted from the Ancient Church Fathers. The Ancient Church Fathers, including disciples of the twelve apostles, were firmly premillennial, pretribulational, and very pro-Israel.

Ancient Book of Jasher
Referenced in Joshua 10:13; 2 Samuel 1:18; 2 Timothy 3:8

There are thirteen ancient history books mentioned and recommended by the Bible. The Ancient Book of Jasher is the only one of the thirteen that still exists. It is referenced in Joshua 10:13; 2 Samuel 1:18; and 2 Timothy 3:8. This volume contains the entire ninety-one chapters plus a detailed analysis of the supposed discrepancies, cross-referenced historical accounts, and detailed charts for ease of use. As with any history book, there are typographical errors in the text but with three consecutive timelines running though the histories, it is very easy to arrive at the exact dates of recorded events. It is not surprising that this ancient document confirms the Scripture and the chronology given in the Hebrew version of the Old Testament, once and for all settling the chronology differences between the Hebrew Old Testament and the Greek Septuagint.

Third Corinthians
Ancient Gnostics and the End of the World

This little known, 2000-year-old Greek manuscript was used in the first two centuries to combat Gnostic cults. Whether or not it is an authentic copy of the original epistle written by the apostle Paul, it gives an incredible look into the cults that will arise in the Last Days. It contains a prophecy that the same heresies that pervaded the first century church would return before the Second Coming of the Messiah.

Ancient Paganism
The Sorcery of the Fallen Angels
Ancient Paganism explores the false religion of the ancient pre-Flood world and its spread into the Gentile nations after Noah's Flood. Quotes from the ancient church fathers, rabbis, and the Talmud detail the activities and beliefs of both Canaanite and New Testament era sorcery. This book explores how, according to biblical prophecy, this same sorcery will return before the Second Coming of Jesus Christ to earth. These religious beliefs and practices will invade the end time church and become the basis for the religion of the Antichrist. Wicca, Druidism, Halloween, Yule, meditation, and occultic tools are discussed at length.

The Rapture
The Pretribulational Rapture of the Church Viewed From the Bible and the Ancient Church
This book presents the doctrine of the pretribulational Rapture of the church. Many prophecies are explored with Biblical passages and terms explained. Evidence is presented that proves the first century church believed the End Times would begin with the return of Israel to her ancient homeland, followed by the Tribulation and the Second Coming. More than fifty prophecies have been fulfilled since Israel became a state. Evidence is also given that several ancient rabbis and at least four ancient church fathers taught a pretribulational Rapture. This book also gives many of the answers to the arguments midtribulationists and posttribulationists use. It is our hope this book will be an indispensable guide for debating the doctrine of the Rapture.

Ancient Epistle of Barnabas
His Life and Teaching
The Epistle of Barnabas is often quoted by the ancient church fathers. Although not considered inspired Scripture, it was used to combat legalism in the first two centuries AD. Besides explaining why the Laws of Moses are not binding on Christians, the Epistle explains how many of the Old Testament rituals teach typological prophecy. Subjects explored are: Yom Kippur, the Red Heifer ritual, animal

sacrifices, circumcision, the Sabbath, Daniel's visions and the end-time ten nation empire, and the temple. The underlying theme is the Three-Fold Witness. Barnabas teaches that mature Christians must be able to lead people to the Lord, testify to others about Bible prophecy fulfilled in their lifetimes, and teach creation history and creation science to guard the faith against the false doctrine of evolution. This is one more ancient church document that proves the first century church was premillennial and constantly looking for the Rapture and other prophecies to be fulfilled.

The Ancient Church Fathers
What the Disciples of the Apostles Taught

This book reveals who the disciples of the twelve apostles were and what they taught, from their own writings. It documents the same doctrine was faithfully transmitted to their descendants in the first few centuries and where, when, and by whom, the doctrines began to change. The ancient church fathers make it very easy to know for sure what the complete teachings of Jesus and the twelve apostles were. You will learn, from their own writings, what the first century disciples taught about the various doctrines that divide our church today. You will learn what was discussed at the seven general councils and why. You will learn who were the cults and cult leaders that began to change doctrine and spread their heresy and how that became to be the standard teaching in the medieval church. A partial list of doctrines discussed in this book are:

Abortion	False gospels
Animal sacrifices	False prophets
Antichrist	Foreknowledge
Arminianism	Free will
Bible or tradition	Gnostic cults
Calvinism	Homosexuality
Circumcision	Idolatry
Deity of Jesus Christ	Islam
Demons	Israel's return
Euthanasia	Jewish food laws
Evolution	Mary's virginity

Mary's assumption	Roman Catholicism
Meditation	The Sabbath
The Nicolaitans	Salvation
Paganism	Schism of Nepos
Predestination	Sin / Salvation
Premillennialism	The soul
Purgatory	Spiritual gifts
Psychology	Transubstantiation
Reincarnation	Yoga
Replacement theology	Women in ministry

Ancient Book of Daniel

The ancient Hebrew prophet Daniel lived in the fifth century BC and accurately predicted the history of the nation of Israel from 536 BC to AD 1948. He also predicted the date of the death of the Messiah to occur in AD 32, the date of the rebirth of the nation of Israel to occur in AD 1948, and the Israeli capture of the Temple Mount to take place in AD 1967! Commentary from the ancient rabbis and the first century church reveals how the messianic rabbis and the disciples of the apostles interpreted his prophecies. Daniel also indicated where the Antichrist would come from, where he would place his international headquarters, and identified the three rebel nations that will attack him during the first three-and-a-half years of the Tribulation.

Ancient Epistles of John and Jude

This book provides commentary for the epistles of John and Jude from the ancient church fathers. It gives the history of the struggles of the first century church. You will learn which cults John and Jude were writing about and be able to clearly identify each heresy. You will also learn what meditation and sorcery truly are. At the end of each chapter is a chart contrasting the teaching of the church and that of the Gnostics. Included are master charts of the doctrine of Christ, the commandments of Christ, and the teaching of the apostles.

Learn the major doctrines that all Christians must believe: Jesus is the only Christ, Jesus is the only Savior, Jesus is the only begotten Son of

God, Jesus is sinless, Jesus physically resurrected, Jesus will physically return to earth, God is not evil, The Rapture, Creationism, Eternal life only by Jesus, The sin nature, Prophecy proves inspiration, Idolatry is evil

Ancient Messianic Festivals,
And The Prophecies They Reveal
The messianic festivals are the biblical rituals God commanded the ancient Israelites to observe. These ancient rites give great detail about the First Coming of the Messiah including the date on which He would arrive, the manner of His death, and the birth of His church. You will also learn of the many disasters that befell the Jews through the centuries on the ninth of Av. The rituals speak of a Natzal, or rapture of believers, and a terrible time called the Yamin Noraim. They give a rather complete outline of this seven-year tribulation period, including the rise of a false messiah. They also tell of a time when the earth will be at peace in the Messianic Kingdom. In addition to the seven messianic festivals, you will learn the prophetic outline of other ceremonies like Hanukkah, the new moon ceremony, the wedding ceremony, the ashes of the red heifer, and the ancient origins of Halloween. You will also learn of other prophetical types and shadows mentioned in the Bible.

Ancient Word of God
Is there a verse missing from your Bible? Would you like to know why it was removed? This book covers the history of the transmission of the Bible text through the centuries. It examines and proves, based on fulfilled Bible prophecy, which Greek texts faithfully preserve the ancient Word of God. You will learn about the first century cults that created their own warped Bibles and of the warnings that the ancient church gave in regard to the pure text. Over two hundred English Bibles are compared. Is the KJV more accurate, maybe the NIV, or perhaps the NASB or ESV?

Cults and the Trinity
This book compares Christianity with the false religions of the world today based on the accuracy of fulfilled Bible prophecy. No other

religion has used prophecy fulfilled in the reader's lifetime to prove its authority, except the Bible. With more than fifty prophecies fulfilled since AD 1948, and Jesus' teaching that He is the only way to salvation, we can conclude we must be a Christian to gain eternal life. Jesus declares you must follow His teachings in order to obtain eternal life. Among these teachings is the fact that Jesus is God incarnate, the second person of the Trinity. Numerous church fathers' quotes dating back to the first century AD show this fact as well, and the ancient church defined a cult as a group claiming to be Christian but denying the Trinity. Listing over one hundred cults and numerous subgroups, this book shows that virtually all of them are nontrinitarians. A detailed, yet simple, study on the Trinity will enable you to witness to all the cults using only this one doctrine.

Ancient Book of Enoch
The Holy Spirit inspired Jude to quote Enoch for a reason. The Ancient Book of Enoch opens by addressing those in the Tribulation period. It contains numerous prophecies about the flood and fire judgments, and the two comings of the Messiah. It teaches that the Messiah is the Son of God and that He will shed His blood to redeem us and even predicts the generation that this would occur!

The book of Enoch prophesies a window of time in which the Second Coming would occur and prophesies that there will be twenty-three Israeli Prime Ministers ruling in fifty-eight terms from AD 1948 to the beginning of the Tribulation period, and much more. Even though it prophecies that the Bible would be created and says we will be judged by our obedience to the Bible, it also makes it clear that this book is not to be added to the Canon of Scripture.

The Ancient Book of Enoch recounts the history of the angels who fell in the days of Jared, Enoch's father. It testifies to their marriages with human women and their genetic experiments. This commentary includes a previously unknown chapter from the Dead Sea Scrolls that actually explains how they did their genetic tampering.

Ancient Epistles of Timothy and Titus
This book provides commentary for the epistles of Timothy and Titus from the ancient church fathers. It describes the history of the struggles of the first century church. It reveals which heretics and cults Paul was writing about. It details the history of those heretics and their errors. Learn which Gnostic cults Alexander, Demas, Hymenaeus, Philetus, Phygellus, and Hermogenes were involved in, what heresies they taught, and exactly why Paul excommunicated them. At the end of each chapter is a chart contrasting the teaching of the church and that of the Gnostics. Included are master charts of sound doctrine, the commandments of Christ, and the teaching of the apostles.

Fallen Angels
Using only the Bible, Dead Sea Scrolls, the writings of the ancient rabbis, and the writings of the ancient church fathers, this book puts together the history of the creation of angelic beings, the fall of Lucifer and his angels, the fall of Azazel, and the fall of Samyaza and his angels. Learn the history of the Nephilim (giants) both pre-flood and post-flood. Find details of many angels, demons, and nephilim in the dictionary at the back of the book. Even find out the exact location on earth of the fallen angel Azazel.

Ancient Book of Jubilees
Almost lost over the centuries, the Book of Jubilees was retrieved from the Ethiopic language and was recently found among the Dead Sea Scrolls. The Book of Jubilees is also called the Little Genesis, Book of Divisions, and the Apocalypse of Moses. It repeats the events of Genesis and Exodus from Creation to the Exodus of the Children of Israel from Egypt. It recounts the events in sets of jubilees (sets of 49 years) and gives additional details such as the fall of the angels, and the creation and destruction of the Nephilim. It also mentions the three classes of pre-flood Nephilim. It details the fact that one-tenth of their disembodied spirits would remain on earth as demons to tempt people and nine-tenths would be chained until the Tribulation Period. Learn what secrets this Dead Sea Scroll holds. Compare the mysterious Qumran calendar with that of the Bible to

learn more about biblical prophecies. The commentary is written from a fundamentalist Christian perspective.

The Gnostic Origins of Calvinism

This book traces the history of Calvinistic thought and its infiltration into the church through the centuries. We start with the Valentinian Gnostics of the first and second centuries and catalog the reaction of the ancient church fathers. We then jump to the Gnostic Manicheans with Augustine and Pelagius in the fifth century AD. Finally, we arrive at Calvin and Knox, who formed modern Calvinism with its acceptance into Protestant thought in the fifteenth century, and the reaction to Calvinism by Jacob Arminius. After looking at the history of Calvinism, we will examine the doctrine of Calvinism and compare it to the doctrines of the Bible and the first century church. Quotes from the church fathers can be read in their entirety in the ten-volume set of *Ante-Nicene Fathers*, and summarized in *Ancient Church Fathers*.

The Gnostic Origins of Roman Catholicism

The ancient church fathers documented their struggle with the rebellion of the bishops of Rome. They recorded the heresies that crept into the Roman Catholic Church and their subsequent rebuke of those Roman bishops, or popes. The first section will give a detailed history of Rome from AD 50 to modern times. The second section will deal with some ancient prophecies about the rise and fall of papal Rome. The third section deals directly with some of the major divisive issues created by the Roman Catholic Church, such as: papal infallibility, idolatry, sorcery, transubstantiation, celibacy, purgatory, etc. The true origin of these doctrinal heresies are the Gnostic cults of the first and second century. Quotes from the church fathers can be read in their entirety in the ten volume set of *Ante-Nicene Fathers*, and summarized in *Ancient Church Fathers*.

For more information visit us at:

Biblefacts.org

Bibliography

Ken Johnson, *Ancient Prophecies Revealed*, Createspace, 2008
Ken Johnson, *Ancient Epistle of Barnabas*, Createspace, 2010
Eerdmans Publishing, *Ante-Nicene Fathers*, Eerdmans Publishing, 1886
Cruse, C. F., *Eusebius' Ecclesiastical History*, Hendrickson Publishers, 1998
Ken Johnson, *Ancient Paganism*, Createspace, 2009
David Bercot, *A Dictionary of Early Christian Beliefs*, Hendrickson Publishers, 1999
Ken Johnson, *Ancient Church Fathers*, Createspace, 2010

Index

Acts of Paul, 89
Acts of Paul and Thecla, 90
Acts of Solomon, 102
Adam and Eve, First Book of, 92
Adam and Eve, Second Book of, 94
Adam, Apocalypse of, 90
Ahijah the Shilonite, Prophecy of, 102
Alcibades, Book of, 91
Alexandrians, Epistle of, 92
Annals of Jehu, 102
Ante-Nicene Church Fathers, 104
Apocalypse of Adam, 90
Apocalypse of Paul, 86
Apocalypse of Peter, 73
Apocalypse of the Virgin, 90
Apocryphon of James, 75
Apocryphon of John, 77
Apostles, Epistle of the, 81
Archons, Hypostasis of the, 93
Ascension of Paul, 90
Barnabas, Epistle of, 103
Barnabas, Gospel of, 46
Book of Alcibades, 91
Book of Enoch, 104
Book of Jasher, 102
Book of Jubilees, 104
Book of Revelations, 91
Book of Samuel the Seer, 102
Book of the Kings, Treatise of, 102
Book of the Wars of the Lord, 102
Book of Thomas the Contender, 78

Chronicles of Gad the Seer, 102
Chronicles of King David, 102
Chronicles of Kings, 102
Corinthians, Third, 103
Dialogue of the Savior, 79
Egyptians, Gospel of the, 48
Enoch, Book of, 104
Enoch, Second, 94
Enoch, Third, 94
Epistle of Alexandrians, 92
Epistle of Barnabas, 103
Epistle of Laodiceans, 92
Epistle of the Apostles, 81
Eusebius, 104
Exegesis on the Soul, 92
First Book of Adam and Eve, 92
Flora, Ptolemy's Letter to, 85
Gad the Seer, Chronicles of, 102
Gospel of Barnabas, 46
Gospel of Judas, 51
Gospel of Mary, 53
Gospel of Peter, 70
Gospel of Philip, 55
Gospel of Pseduo-Matthew, 59
Gospel of the Egyptians, 48
Gospel of the Hebrews, 69
Gospel of the Nativity of Mary, 69
Gospel of Thomas, 60
Gospel of Truth, 63
Gospels, Infancy, 65
Hebrews, Gospel of the, 69
Hermas, Shepherd of, 95
History of Joseph the Carpenter, 70
Hypostasis of the Archons, 93
Iddo the prophet, Treatise of, 102
Infancy Gospels, 65

James, Apocryphon of, 75
James, Protevangelium of, 67
James, Secret Book of, 75
Jasher, Book of, 102
Jehu, Annals of, 102
Jesus Christ, Sophia of, 88
John, Apocryphon of, 77
John, Secret Book of, 77
Joseph the Carpenter, History of, 70
Joseph, Prayer of, 69
Josephus, 103
Jubilees, Book of, 104
Judas, Gospel of, 51
King David, Chronicles of, 102
Laodiceans, Epistle of, 92
Letter of Peter to Philip, 83
Mark, Secret Gospel of, 69
Mary, Gospel of, 53
Melchizedek, 93
Nathan the Prophet, Records of, 102
Nativity of Mary, Gospel of the, 69
New Book of Psalms, 93
On the Origin of the World, 93
Paul and Thecla, Acts of, 90
Paul, Acts of, 89
Paul, Apocalypse of, 86
Paul, Ascension of, 90
Paul, Revelation of, 86
Paul, Vision of, 86
Peter, Apocalypse of, 73
Peter, Gospel of, 70
Peter, Preaching of, 96
Peter, Revelation of, 73
Peter, Teaching of, 96
Philip, Gospel of, 55
Philip, Letter of Peter to, 83

Pistis Sophia, 84
Prayer of Joseph, 69
Preaching of Peter, 96
Prophecy of Ahijah the Shilonite, 102
Protevangelium of James, 67
Psalms, New Book of, 93
Pseduo-Matthew, Gospel of, 59
Ptolemy's Letter to Flora, 85
Records of Nathan the Prophet, 102
Revelation of Paul, 86
Revelation of Peter, 73
Revelations, Book of, 91
Samuel the Seer, Book of, 102
Savior, Dialogue of the, 79
Sayings of the Seers, 102
Second Book of Adam and Eve, 94
Second Enoch, 94
Secret Book of James, 75
Secret Book of John, 77
Secret Gospel of Mark, 69
Seder Olam, 103
Seers, Sayings of, 102
Sentences of Sextus, 95
Sextus, Sentences of, 95
Shepherd of Hermas, 95
Solomon, Acts of, 102
Sophia of Jesus Christ, 88
Teaching of Peter, 96
Third Corinthians, 103
Third Enoch, 94
Thomas the Contender, Book of, 78
Thomas, Gospel of, 60
Treatise of the Book of the Kings, 102
Treatise of the Prophet Iddo, 102
Tripartite Tractate, 97
Truth, Gospel of, 63

Virgin, the Apocalypse of, 90
Vision of Paul, 86
Wars of the Lord, Book of, 102

Printed in Great Britain
by Amazon